Rose

I hope this book helps and guides you along your Spiritual journey of growth! :)

Lots of Love

allia x x

Sha'ban Ramadan Shawwal

A guide to nurturing the soul during these blessed months

Nabeelah Niaz

Ta-Ha Publishers Ltd.

First Published in February 2024

by: Ta-Ha Publishers Ltd,
Unit 4, The Windsor Centre,
Windsor Grove, London, SE27 9NT
United Kingdom
www.tahapublishers.com
support@tahapublishers.com

Written by: Nabeelah Niaz
Editor: Arooj Rashid Hussain
Cover/Book design and Typesetting: Shakir Abdulcadir

A catalogue record of this book is available from the British Library
ISBN: 978-1-915357-32-8 (Hardback)
10 9 8 7 6 5 4 3 2 1

Printed and bound by: IMAK Ofset, Türkiye

بسم الله الرحمن الرحيم

In the name of Allah ﷾,
The most Merciful, The most Compassionate

Peace and blessings upon
our Prophet Muhammad ﷺ, the best of mankind

Contents

Author's note

Rewind to fifteen years earlier:
I'm a new mother with two children; I'm a wife, a daughter and a friend. I have a full-time job to hold down and am always seeking ways to better myself as a Muslim. There are so many things to juggle at the moment, and the month of Ramadan is fast approaching...does this sound familiar?

No matter what our situation is, maintaining a strong connection with Allah ﷾ during Ramadan while simultaneously juggling all of our responsibilities and goals is *not* easy.

If you're a parent, the children still need dropping off and picking up from school. As an adult, the cooking, cleaning, ironing and washing still need to be done, but you also want to carve out time for a healthy social life. You want to dedicate some quality time to either your spouse, your parents, your family members and/or your friends, all while yearning for a consistently deep and peaceful spiritual connection during Ramadan.

If you're a student, the homework, coursework and exam preparation is a never-ending reality. You want to succeed at work, but also need time for yourself to relax, decompress and unwind after a demanding and stressful day.

There are not enough hours in the day, so how are we going to truly be able to make the most of the barakah of Ramadan and hit the pause button?

We often view Ramadan as a chance to cleanse ourselves spiritually, mentally and physically, and therefore feel disheartened when we realise we haven't developed these aspects of ourselves as deeply as we would have liked to.

Ever since I was a child, I have fasted. It was something I always knew I had to do as a young Muslim. Some years I was more focused than others, with happy and sad moments along the way. Each year, I'd have some form of regret that I could have done better and, at times, I felt quite disconnected and disappointed with myself.

I would make the intention to continue to pray regularly, to read and reflect on the Qur'an more. In later years, I made the intention to socialise with like-minded friends that encourage each other to become better believers, parents, spouses, children to our parents, and positive role models.

Guaranteed, I would have the best of intentions to keep up the positive changes beyond Ramadan. But the month would finish, and I'd feel exhausted. My efforts would start to decrease, and before I knew it, my connection with Allah ﷻ would feel weaker.

In the back of our minds, we know we can muster up enough strength to get through thirty days of dedicated religiosity, but then we fall back into what life was like before Ramadan. We naturally become distracted by our routines and busy schedules again, leaving those beautiful practices we worked so hard to implement behind in Ramadan as a bittersweet, nostalgic memory.

Months later, I'd be in denial, wondering how I let that happen. Why did I let go of my efforts so easily?

I'd feel regretful and question my ability to be a good Muslim in Allah's Eyes ﷻ. The cycle would repeat year after year. I'd pray that I would be guided and that this cycle would stop.

Then I learnt more about the importance of the months of Sha'ban and Shawwal, that nestle around Ramadan, and realised why my spiritual development always felt restricted. I realised that adopting a 'Ramadan mindset' meant that I wasn't looking at the bigger picture.

Fast forward to ten years later:
Allah ﷻ made me realise that He does not change the condition of a people until we want to change it ourselves, and that healthy growth is achieved by good practices that are small, frequent and meaningful over time. We have to believe and plan that we have the power to break the cycle and create good, lasting habits that can benefit us at a deeper, individual level.

As with learning any new skill or art form, long- term spiritual growth requires practising skills little by little every day to see their positive results. Limiting all efforts to thirty days is neither healthy or sustainable for strong spiritual growth in the long term.

I'm still imperfect, human and have a long way to go, but the important thing is that I keep trying. There are times when I can't help feeling that so many years have been wasted. But I can't change the past, so why waste more time dwelling on it? At times, it's easier said than done; however, there is so much to learn and achieve as a Muslim. I know that help and guidance comes from Allah ﷾ alone. I seek His help and know that His plan is better than mine.

I'd like to share the strategies that have benefitted me over the years in developing a more ***sustained*** spiritual connection with Allah ﷾; the practices that have helped me become closer to Him leading up to, during ***and*** after the beautiful and blessed month of Ramadan.

Whether you are studying at school or university, working young adults, single, married, or parents with children, there's practical guidance here for everyone in this book.

> It's never too late to start planting little seeds of good, spiritual practice now, so that no matter what rain or shine you experience in life, you are destined to bloom.

Habits don't form overnight

Allah سُبْحَانَهُ وَتَعَالَىٰ does not change the condition of a people until we want to change it ourselves

Everyone has their own journey, it's not a competition – it's continual development

The key is to start small and take one step at a time

Implement small actions of goodness every day until it feels like an integrated, normal practice

When striving for growth in any aspect of yourself, make a sincere intention and ask Allah ﷻ to guide you in your endeavour(s). The barakah of this will make it easier for you, insha'Allah

Your seeds
SHA'BAN

This is the month to **prepare** ourselves spiritually, mentally and physically—the month to start sowing the positive seeds, and to begin creating the right **environment** for growth and change.

Think about the type of spiritual growth you want to see in the much-awaited month of Ramadan. How are you going to create the right 'environment', 'temperature' and 'lighting' for the seeds of your connection with Allah ﷻ to start blossoming?

This is a powerful analogy to remember for your own spiritual growth during the blessed month. Think about what you want your spiritual growth to look like during and beyond Ramadan.

Do you want your connection with Allah سبحانه وتعالى, much like a plant, to be seasonal (**short term growth**) and limited only to one holy month? Or do you want a connection that sustains and grows healthily beyond the month of Ramadan (**long term growth**)?

If we wish to achieve the healthier, long term growth, your first steps ('seeds') will therefore need to be planted ***before*** Ramadan, in the month of Sha'ban.

How could you start to implement small, good practices in the weeks leading up to Ramadan to enable you to truly flourish within it, and beyond?

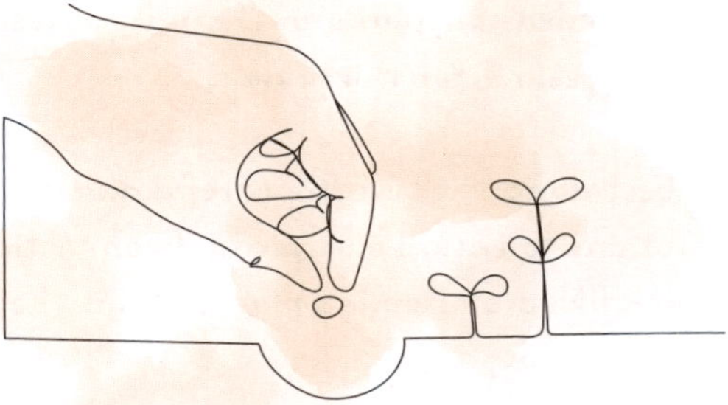

Your sustenance
RAMADAN

This is the month of nurturing and feeding your soul.

In this sacred month, we begin to really feel the joys of our renewed spiritual growth and are keen to maintain this feeling for thirty days.

This is best done when we are careful and attentive with our actions to ensure our spiritual connection thrives, much like a blossoming plant, and is the healthiest it can be.

Keep nourishing your soul, little by little. Do not give up on your efforts.

Like a plant's roots that become overwhelmed and weakened by overwatering at once, we need to be careful with our additional acts of worship during Ramadan, and beyond.

Striving to achieve absolutely everything in your fasting day while aiming for a perfect, well-rounded Ramadan will mean you are likely to exhaust yourself. Often, that mental exhaustion leads to a spiritual exhaustion. Setting high expectations is commendable, but remember to be kind to yourself. Be selective with what you do with your time, just like disciplining the amount of water given to a plant in a day. This way, you will have the mental space and drive to maintain a healthier connection with Allah ﷾; you can truly embrace the mercies of Ramadan and connect more deeply.

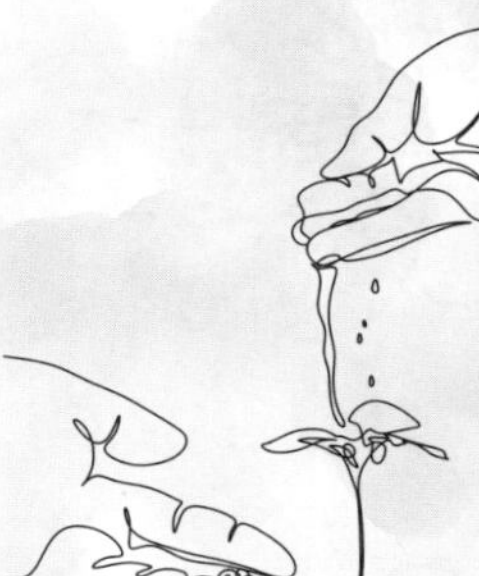

It is the *quality* of your connection, not the quantity of your extra, voluntary practices that cultivates a *healthy* spiritual growth.

Your renewal
SHAWWAL

Welcome to Shawwal. The beautiful habits we have worked so hard to nurture over the last two months are in full bloom.

Your spiritual connection with Allah ﷻ is feeling healthier than ever, insha'Allah, and you want to hold on to that special feeling of contentment for as long as possible.

Keep nourishing that connection by maintaining those good practices. Pray that your growth is even better than last year. Let this be the year where your closeness to Allah ﷾ thrives and survives against the test of time.

Life in this world is full of challenges and tests; these will keep coming—but we are now so much better equipped to face them as we have become truly strengthened from within.

Our bond with Allah ﷾ feels more resilient, strong, and firmly planted. We have tasted our own potential to be the best version of ourselves.

Beauty lies in the reality that we can only get better every year.

So let's keep trying.

If you remain firmly rooted in your faith, you will eventually see the beautiful fruits of your perseverance.

No one will reap except what they sow.

(Al-An'am, 6:164)

Ibn 'Umar رضي الله عنهما reported that our Prophet Muhammed ﷺ said: *"There is a tree amongst trees, the leaves of which do not wither and that is like a Muslim; it resembles a faithful believer..."* (Bukhari)

Opening prayer

- I pray to Allah ﷻ that we make sincere intentions in becoming more God-conscious in the month of the Sha'ban, and that we plant seeds (implement good practices) in this month that will enable our closeness with Allah to develop, and our attainment of His mercy to flourish before we reach Ramadan.

- I pray that during Ramadan, our drive to attain a stronger connection with Allah ﷻ continues to flourish, and we are attentive to the many blessings and rewards (barakah) this brings to our lives. I pray that we use our days and nights as a time of deep introspection, and are able to fulfil this pillar of our religion to the best of our ability. I pray that we use this sacred month as a time of sustenance for the soul—an opportunity to hit pause and think about how we can strengthen our closeness with Allah سبحانه وتعالى from within ourselves and through others.

- I pray that we continue to strengthen the good habits we have worked hard to instil, no matter how big or small, into Shawwal and beyond. I pray that we can become more ***mindful*** in our spiritual practices, focusing on nourishing ourselves from ***within*** to help us attain a resilient, thriving and enduring connection with our Lord, rather than completing practices for short term goals and rewards.

Ameen

Sha'ban – A new beginning

Sha'ban is the month that nestles in between Rajab and Ramadan, some of the most revered months in the Islamic calendar. The importance of Sha'ban is often overlooked, but to our beloved Prophet Muhammad ﷺ, Sha'ban was an incredibly significant month of worship leading up to Ramadan.

In the days leading up to the beginning of Ramadan, we may often find ourselves spending time practically preparing our kitchen cupboards and freezers for our upcoming iftar (sunset meal) nights, or scheduling our 'last treat' meals before the fasting month is officially upon us. We might start to binge-watch our favourite Netflix series, knowing that in Ramadan we won't be watching much TV. However, it is important to note that the significance of the month of Sha'ban has been emphasised in the sunnah as a **warm up** to Ramadan, a time for spiritual preparation—in mind, body and soul. While the month of Ramadan is indeed a sacred time of year for Muslims, Prophet Muhammad ﷺ stressed on giving Sha'ban its due diligence.

Usama ibn Zaid ؓ said:

O Messenger of Allah, I do not see you fasting any month as much as Sha'ban. He said, "That is a month to which people do not pay much attention, between Rajab and Ramadan. It is a month in which the deeds are taken up to the Lord of the worlds, and I like that my deeds be taken up when I am fasting." (Nasa'i)

So, aside from performing additional fasts,

why is Sha'ban so important?

Let's take a scenario. When we have an exam, a job interview, a promotion, an important family gathering or an event, how do we prepare for it so that we succeed, and get the results that we desire? When we work hard for this, do we not often feel a sense of achievement once it is all done, knowing that we tried our best?

Let's now take one of these examples and apply it to the month of Sha'ban:

If we have an exam in a month's time, despite our best efforts to plan in advance, most of us end up revising at the last minute, cramming everything in and causing ourselves stress and exhaustion. We then become too exhausted to continue with anything else afterward. Having said this, we all know that if we had a plan, revised a little at a time each day, we could avoid all of the last minute pressure and would feel more confident too.

The month of Sha'ban is no different.

It's a month that increases your chances to succeed in Ramadan. The more you actively and mentally prepare within this month, the more it decreases the chances of regret and disappointment.

Success is rarely an accident and more often the result of a well-defined plan with small, effective and consistent actions. It's a month where the Companions of the Prophet ﷺ would secretly fast and strive. With this in mind, let's strive together so that we too can become amongst the forerunners in the next world.

We will now go through some practical tips about how you can feasibly get the most out of Sha'ban—whether you are male or female, studying, working, or parenting—and what habits you can implement to help make this a spiritually rewarding month for you and your family. To aid our growth, there are sections on:

- Preparing the heart and mind
- Preparing the body
- Preparing our environment

Preparing the heart and mind

Intention

First of all, make a sincere commitment and intention to start preparing for success in Sha'ban to help yourself be the best that you can be, to help those around you grow, and to positively influence each other towards goodness. It doesn't matter if Ramadan is a month away. Allah ﷻ knows all of your intentions.

'Umar ibn al-Khattab ؓ narrated that Allah's Messenger ﷺ said: *"The reward of deeds depends upon the intentions and every person will get the reward according to what he has intended."* (Bukhari)

The first step to this growth is your intention: pray to Allah ﷻ to help you in your journey towards becoming closer to Him—a journey to earn His pleasure. Renew your wudu for the next prayer, and ask Allah ﷻ to guide you and give you the strength to move forward. When you are praying, think of the words in Surah al-Fatihah where we say:

It is You we serve and it is You we ask for help

In seeking Allah's ﷾ help and guidance to help make these positive, spiritual habits easier for you to establish, your growth will manifest in ways that are better than you imagined, insha'Allah. This is the power of a sincere intention.

Now we've renewed our intention to make positive efforts, we can spend some time in the month of Sha'ban to declutter the mind and create a productive environment for spiritual growth. For this, it is important to begin with a clean heart.

Asking for forgiveness

As you ask Allah ﷾ to help you on your journey to success, ask openly for His forgiveness, so that you can move forward with a pure heart—this will help you start your spiritual growth with a promising, clean slate. Don't be frugal in your request for forgiveness—generously pour your heart into your prostrations, at the end of your prayers and during the day, and pray for purification. For isn't the best growth bound to happen when the roots are refined and strengthened?

As you strive for purification in preparation for a successful month of Ramadan, don't forget that resolving any big or small issue with family and friends is equally an important part of this process in Sha'ban.

This can sometimes be difficult, so here are some strategies you can use to help you achieve this:

- Make a list of the people that you have unresolved issues with—make an intention to clear the air with them before the blessed month of Ramadan.

- Make du'a that Allah ﷻ can forgive you and them, and that Allah ﷻ guides you both to goodness in this life and the next. Making a supplication for the one that you have fallen out with is a great act of humility that Allah سبحانه وتعالى admires greatly. So if this is the least you can do, what is there to lose? Remember that we should strive to treat people mercifully, in the way we would want the world, and our Lord, to treat us.

- Remind yourself of at least one thing you can respect about this person whom you have become estranged from, like a time when they showed up for you and supported you, even if it was in the past. Is there anything that you may have said or done to them that would have displeased Allah سبحانه وتعالى? Even if you are not sure, ask forgiveness from Allah سبحانه وتعالى for this anyway, and be sincere in your repentance, for Allah سبحانه وتعالى knows you better than you know yourself.

- Allah Almighty is Al-Rahim, All Merciful, and if He can forgive the most sinful, why can't we extend an ounce of this mercy to a brother or sister in our Ummah? In Allah's Eyes سبحانه وتعالى, we are all worthy of forgiveness, so let's forgive and move on with our lives, without unresolved conflicts, in the hope that Allah سبحانه وتعالى is pleased with our humility, and extends His forgiveness to us in our time of need.

- Even if you firmly believe you are not in the wrong and have been deeply hurt by somebody's actions, can you find it in yourself to be a role model by trying to make things right, or at least clear the air? You do not necessarily need to be close or even friends; in fact, you can forgive and move forward in separate directions. The very act of releasing each other from this burden of unresolved conflict/tension is a relief in itself that will eventually lead to a state of peace (sukoon) and contentment, insha'Allah. These long term gratifications are worth the difficult conversations. Growth rarely occurs in our comfort zones.

- Be mindful that sometimes things are said whilst a person may have struggles going on behind closed doors that we are unaware of.

- Alternatively, you could even try calling them and seeing if they are willing to meet up in Sha'ban. Often, people are understandably fearful of rejection and are therefore afraid to make the first move, when the reality is that they would like to make amends. Extending that olive branch might just be the signal they were waiting for. You won't know unless you try. You could invite them to your home, or arrange to meet in a neutral place with a mutual friend, if this feels more comfortable for you.

- We know that we cannot control everything—the outcomes of our efforts are ultimately in Allah's Hands ﷿; but we know that our honourable intentions and efforts will *never* go unnoticed by Him. It could be that you reach out and the person is not interested in making amends. Allah ﷿ is Al-Sami' and Al-Basir, The All-Hearing and All-Seeing; He hears and sees all of our noble efforts, be they in the open or in private. So never consider your efforts as futile in this world, as they are being accounted for by our Lord and will increase you in rank in the afterlife.

- Your own heart will be cleansed and your mind put at ease by knowing that you had the wisdom to act honourably in a difficult situation.

> **Each soul is responsible for its own actions; no soul will bear the burden of another. Your goal in the end is towards Allah: He will inform you of that in which you differed.** (Al-An'am, 6:164)

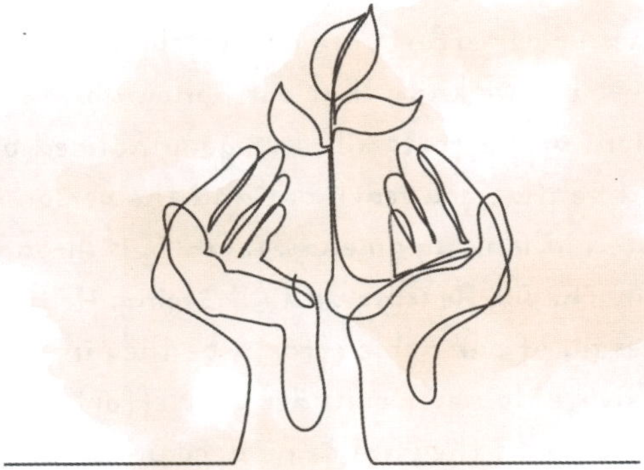

❀ When seeking to cleanse your heart from prior disagreements that have upset you, supplicate in earnest to Allah ﷾, by using His empowering names. For example, when I am in the situation where I feel that I've upset someone, or someone has upset me, I pray in my prostration. I call upon Allah ﷾ using one of His Names—Al-Jaami'—The Uniter. I pray that He unites me with those that are upset and brings us together. I pray that He softens our hearts towards one another, clears up any misunderstandings and shortcomings between us, and removes any grudges and envy, so that our hearts are ready and purified.

Ameen

Disconnect

One of the things that unites many of us is our dependency on social media. Social media can be a great source of knowledge and information; a way to stay connected with people in our community, and a medium for raising awareness about important causes. However, balance is essential to a healthy spiritual growth.

If we're not disciplined with the time we spend on social media, we can easily become addicted to scrolling through content that might not always be good for our soul. It's so easy to lose track of time on social media, due to its endlessness of posts and stories. Let's carefully consider this:

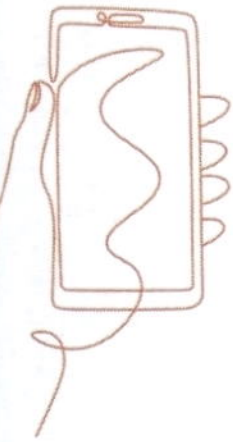

How much of what we actually see and do on social media is purposeful? Are we posting for attention, or with good intention? Are we casually following, liking and thereby advocating sinful content? Are we using our social media to feed our nafs, ego, or sense of privilege? Or are we using it **with heart**, to serve a greater purpose?

Use the month of Sha'ban to more seriously start questioning your intention behind and level of engagement with social media. Create some time to **'disconnect' in order to connect** with other aspects of your spiritual growth. Your reduction of social media time doesn't have to be radical, as habits are hard to break; implementing even the smallest changes can create powerful ripples.

So believe in yourself—you have what it takes to be selective in how you connect and disconnect, and what people's feeds you choose to follow. YOU are in control of your actions. And if you tell yourself enough that you have what it takes to use social media more consciously, then Allah ﷻ will help you achieve this. The first step is a sincere intention.

You may decide by the time you reach Ramadan to take a complete break from social media. If you are struggling with this and find it impossible to disconnect, then allocate yourself some structured social media time in the day, and scroll wisely.

Filter what you see and who you follow in order to cleanse your social media exposure. There are so many beautiful posts, videos, motivational reminders, du'as and inspirational role models in our world that we can learn from and share posts about in the month of Sha'ban—distilling your searches to these examples would not only help you prepare mentally for a wholesome Ramadan, it will position you for success beyond it too, insha'Allah.

***

Making attempts to purify your heart and declutter your mind in this way will help you get into the Sha'ban Zone. It will help create the right environment for a beautiful, spiritual growth in the coming months, insha'Allah.

Preparing the body

Food Intake

Part of preparing for a spiritually successful and productive Ramadan also requires a careful balance in diet, for worship of Allah ﷻ is as physiological as it is psychological.

If we want to nurture a ***healthy*** spiritual growth, we should be nourishing ourselves with a certain level of discipline leading up to Ramadan. What we eat and how we eat it should be in proportion to the essential nutrients our body requires in order to flourish in such a spiritually active month. Echoing the analogy of the plant, if we over-fertilise it, it can cause harm to the root system, impacting its growth over time.

Remarkably, by the Qadr of Allah ﷻ, our bodies are much the same. Eating excessively and indulgently before Ramadan prepares us less successfully for this active period of supplication, giving rise to lethargy and weakness, which in turn will slow down our spiritual stamina—something we should avoid compromising in this sacred month of worship.

We can utilise Sha'ban as an opportunity to cleanse our bodies by pacing ourselves with our food intake and being more conscious of what we eat, so that by the time Ramadan starts, there is a seamless transition in our practice of daily fasting, rather than one that initially induces the body to the shock of change. This mindset of healthy discipline from the outset will reduce the headaches and fatigue that can occur in the first few days of Ramadan, insha'Allah.

Miqdam ibn Madikarib ﷺ narrated
that I heard the Messenger of Allah ﷺ say:
"A human being fills no worse vessel than his stomach. It is sufficient for a human being to eat a few mouthfuls to keep his spine straight. But if he must (fill it), then one third of food, one third for drink and one third for air." (Ibn Majah)

We frequently hear about this reminder during Ramadan. But many of us feel this is easier said than done, so here are some practical and subtle changes you could begin making to your diet in Sha'ban to help you achieve a smoother transition into your Ramadan fasts:

- Replace soft drinks and caffeine with water and more natural fruit juices.

- Begin to slow down the frequency of your snacking throughout the day, even if it is for a few days a week, so that your body starts to acclimatise to the fasting mindset.

- However, this will only be feasible if your main meals contain healthy, well-rounded ingredients, so plan for more protein-based main meals that will keep you full and active during the day.

- If you do wish to snack in between your meals, opt for healthy fruits and natural sugars, rather than food rich in e-numbers.

- When grocery shopping, look for healthy, high-energy snack options such as nuts, dates, fresh fruits—including cherry tomatoes; bitesize vegetables and dip, like cucumber, carrot or celery sticks, and dried fruits, like raisins.

- Who said healthy food couldn't be tasty? Whether it's a delicious fruit smoothie, a yoghurt and granola bowl with your favourite toppings that are all rich with vitamins, porridge, or chia seeds soaked in milk with strawberries or raspberries, there are plenty of good options for a healthy breakfast or snack that would keep you going during the day.

- If you find a meal or snack that you like, which successfully fills you up and energises you throughout the day, you know you can turn to these ideas for suhoor (pre-dawn meal) in Ramadan.

- You may wish to have a few days of intermittent fasting, where you leave larger gaps between your meals, setting specific meal times on those days to adjust your diet. You could achieve this by either having a late, nutritious breakfast, followed by healthy snacks in the afternoon (or a very light lunch), and then one balanced, evening meal.

- If you can manage it, you could implement the sunnah of fasting on a Monday or a Thursday, or the three White days (13th–15th) of the month to help get you in the Ramadan Zone.

- For sisters that still need to make up a few fasts from menstruation, the month of Sha'ban would be a perfect opportunity to make them up.

Preparing our environment

Here I share ideas about what you can implement in your homes, workplaces, social circles and communities to help you in your growth journey to achieve your best Ramadan.

The workplace/educational institutions

Whether you are working, or studying at school, college or university, it is important to think about what small changes you may need to make during your working day to prepare you for a sustainable and positive Ramadan experience. In a world where diversity and inclusion are at the height of importance, don't be shy in discussing your upcoming Ramadan experience with leaders within your institution, and respectfully voice any important requests in advance of Ramadan to accommodate for your needs during that month—for example, requesting a space to pray at a certain time. However, you must make sure that any requests you do have are within reason, and not at the disadvantage of your colleagues, for we must not let our blessed month be a burden for others. The very least we could achieve from these discussions is educating our institutions about the month of Ramadan and its innumerable benefits, so that the value of Ramadan is shared among our work colleagues.

Tips on what you can do to help and motivate each other:

- Make an effort to network and open up channels of communication with your Muslim brothers and sisters at your institution, and wish each other a blessed Sha'ban.

- Share useful information with each other leading up to and during Ramadan. You can share motivational quotes and information about charity events, and/or extend your kindness by offering dates for their first fast.

- Arrange to pray together if that is a possibility.

- Schedule short breaks at the start of the prayer window to check in with each other. You may not always be able to do this depending on your schedules, but the effort to do so sometimes might go a long way for one your Muslim colleagues.

- If you feel you don't have a Muslim community at your work, don't give up on practising your beliefs. Your Ramadan won't be any short of barakah if you have the best of intentions for the people around you. You should extend the beautiful values of Sha'ban and Ramadan with your non-Muslim work friends with acts of kindness, considered speech and patience.

- For those who may be feeling nervous about establishing salah within their workplace, here is a note of reassurance: when I first started to pray outside of my home, I would feel awkward and would be worried about somebody walking in on me praying. The only way I overcame this was to ask Allah ﷻ directly for the confidence, guidance and strength to fulfil my duties. The reality is it doesn't matter what people think and how they might judge us—we are often our own worst critics. Allah ﷻ is the best Judge and sees all our efforts, despite our own anxieties. I've found through my personal experience that praying outside the home opens up conversations about Islam and our beliefs, so there are more positives that come from trying to establish your practices of faith at work. As with most things in life, we won't know unless we try.

- For those of you that are not working outside of the home, you too will have to plan to get the most out of your days. House tasks are never-ending, so plan in some needed one-to-one time with your Lord just after your salah, and prioritise your spiritual connection over chores that are not immediately urgent.

- Set reminders or alarms on your phone to signal your prayer times, so you don't lose track of your salah in your busy day—try and plan your daily tasks around those times.

Practice makes permanent

Social Interactions

In order to plant the seeds for a healthy, social mindset, it's important to manage our efforts in striving for good and our daily responsibilities.

Take advantage of the blessed months and exert yourself more than you normally would, but not to the extent that you fall and can't pick yourself back up—balance is essential for healthy spiritual growth.

There are a number of ways you can weave spiritual connection into your day in a more holistic way, without tiring yourself out. Whether you are studying, have a job, or are busy with commitments at home, we can reflect carefully on how we could spend our time with others to create barakah rather than spiritual fatigue.

Adults

- If you are getting bored and restless on your own, and are finding that you are scrolling for hours on social media to pass the time, could you spend at least five to ten minutes reading and reflecting on a part of the Qur'an and its translation? Translation apps work well in the absence of a physical Qur'an. (You could do the same thing if you needed some quiet time to yourself to zone out from your day's social activities.) Reading beneficial content is also an invaluable time-pass, as well as listening to insightful Islamic podcasts.

- If you are meeting up with your friends just before Ramadan, could you help steer conversations away from backbiting and unsympathetic comments, and focus instead on gratitude for the innumerable mercies and blessings of Allah ﷻ? Remind yourself that only Allah ﷻ is the true Judge of people.

- Could you focus your conversations on each other's well-being and the goals you have set for your own betterment, rather than commenting disparagingly about the actions of other people, especially if they are not with you to defend themselves?

- If you are living with your family, can you plan for a more collaborative Ramadan at home by sharing out the workload and devising an agreed rota to ensure everyone is happy, so one person does not feel overburdened with responsibilities? Ramadan is an opportunity for the whole family to spiritually grow *together*. Maybe you can help each other with the shopping or cleaning? If you have offered to help, did you say it in earnest and follow up on your offering?

- Spend some time checking in on each other's needs and well-being, rather than just focusing on others' responsibilities and duties, and the short-term results of their actions.

- If you live with your parents/elders, is there anything that you can help them with to relieve them of their burdens?

- If you are parents, what positive messages and habits could you start to instil in your children leading up to Ramadan? Could you be a better role model for them by teaching by example?

- How can you create excitement in your home so that the children look forward to Ramadan, rather than seeing it as a month where they can't do the things they might ordinarily do?

- Could you make a chart or visual tracker with them, so that they can tick off tasks each day? Offer meaningful incentives to them (such as stickers, playtime, reading together time) as rewards for their efforts.

- How can you make Eid al-Fitr a special day of celebration, whilst still incorporating continued worship?

- Is there any way you can educate and bring Muslims together in the workplace, even if it is by kindly offering food?

- Is there anything you could do to help your local mosque in preparation for Ramadan, such as offering them your expertise, or offering to help out with an upcoming event?

Families

- What spiritual activity could you implement together as a family more? Could you read salah together? Or spend five to ten minutes a couple of times in the week watching an Islamic short video, or sharing an inspiring book?

- If you or a member of your house are struggling to pray, can you set alarms for each one?

- If you pray regularly, can you remind each other at home to pray at the beginning of the time window for that salah to support them in their journey to consistency?

- Can you encourage each other to read extra voluntary prayers within your five daily prayers? What about an additional one for wudu, gratitude and/or repentance at least once a week?

- Could you encourage a shared reading of the Qur'an? For example, collectively read a verse from the Qur'an about the upcoming month of Ramadan and reflect upon it, discussing what it means to you when you read it. Or, if you have older children, could you task each other to read different parts by a certain time, and share the lessons and their reflections from it with each other? There are a handful of verses in the Qur'an relating to Ramadan, so you could cover these in the month of Sha'ban.

- If your children need to learn how to pray their salah, or need to revisit this again (recommended), can you help them with this?

- I often find that going over practices that you may have learnt as a child *with* your children is a good way to keep in check the accuracy of your practices—we are all human and sometimes get into habits that might prevent us from fulfilling a task with excellence. So having honest discussions about this as a family is a great way to remind ourselves that:
  - We are all a work in progress, and
  - Progress is made when we make the sincere intention and effort to try.

Students

- Could you arrange a gathering that you feel will distract you from your Ramadan intentions until *after* the Shawwal period, and explain to your peers the reason for this?

- If you would like some company and something different to do in your free time, could you attend or help out at an Islamic event within your school or local community, or the Islamic society at your college/university? If you don't have an Islamic society, could you help organise one? Or, could you help pitch an idea for hosting a charity event for Ramadan, if there is interest?

- If you are speaking with your friends through social media, could you motivate each other by sharing helpful messages and useful ways to improve ourselves during Sha'ban in preparation for Ramadan, rather than falling into habits of bad language and derogatory 'banter'?

- Could you be a role model for someone younger than you? For example, could you help your younger siblings learn how to pray, and help refine their Islamic practice?

- Could you teach a friend or family member a valuable lesson or technique that you have learnt that could help elevate the spiritual knowledge of others? You may have either learnt these during your time at the mosque, through your own wider reading, or from somebody else.

- If you live with your parents/carers, could you spend a few minutes helping them around the house?

- Could you help them prepare for dinner by getting glasses of water ready, or get a few dates out for all of you at the time of opening your fast?

- Is there anything else your parents/carers would appreciate you doing more, such as keeping your room clean, or picking up your plates after eating? Every little bit goes a long way!

- Could you extend your kindness further through voluntary acts of help that they might not ask for themselves?

- Spend quality time with your parents/carers and elders to really treasure the spirit of Ramadan—learn from them; make du'a for their eternal success; speak to them kindly and lovingly; do not patronise them;

be patient with them as they have provided for you since you were a child.

- ❀ You never know what blessed Ramadan may be your/their last, so put in the effort to express any anxieties, struggles or goals each of you may have about your spiritual growth, regardless of your age, being more sensitive to each other's needs.

Within your social circles

- ❀ If you are meeting up with your friends or relatives during Sha'ban, Ramadan or Shawwal, could you share the positive changes you are making leading up to Ramadan with your friends, so that they feel motivated to enhance their own connection with Allah ﷻ, and observe Ramadan more mindfully within their families?

- Could you ask your friends how they plan to better prepare for Ramadan this year? Do any of your friends need some motivation, or know of any particularly useful resources, advice or examples they could share?

- If you have a social gathering arranged during Sha'ban, could you spend some time talking about any positive impact you have felt or seen already from the changes you, or others are implementing?

- Be equally open about your struggles too, if you feel comfortable to talk about these with your friends. Is there anything distracting you or posing a challenge to the growth you wish to achieve over Ramadan? How could we positively overcome this so that we are able to reach our full potential for the sake of Allah ﷻ? Provide solace to those feeling disconnected or lacking confidence in their own self-development. Ramadan is the perfect time to reconnect with our Lord, and you will be rewarded even if you try to gently guide someone who isn't able to plan for a productive Ramadan as well as you might be. One of the best ways to offer your help to a friend is by making sincere du'a for them.

- Sisters, are there any missed fasts you need to make up in Sha'ban due to menstruation? Could you encourage each other to complete these, or observe them together?

Feeding the fasting

Fasting in Ramadan with the rest of our Ummah creates a great community spirit and it's nice to share our experiences with those close to us. Some of us will be invited by friends and family to open our fast, and some of us may wish to host ourselves.

Zaid ibn Khalid al-Juhani ﷺ narrated that the Prophet ﷺ said: *"Whoever gives food for a fasting person to break his fast, he will have a reward like theirs, without that detracting from their reward in the slightest."* (Ibn Majah)

What a beautiful blessing this is. Here are a few handy tips I've learned over the last few years for you to start thinking about in Sha'ban:

- Plan when you want to host. I personally avoid hosting in the last ten nights of Ramadan when we generally all want to exert ourselves in worship. If you do want to open fasts for other people in the last nights, then you could distribute food instead.

- If you are hosting, set a menu that is time-efficient and leads to little wastage. You shouldn't have to spend all day in the kitchen; the more time you spend in the kitchen, the less time you have to focus on the more spiritual aspects of your fast.

- Hosting iftar brings people together, so embrace this spirit by delegating tasks within your household or social circle. Spread the work fairly so that you are not overwhelmed with having to do it all yourself. A positive team spirit contributes to a more nurturing Ramadan experience.

- Remember, hosting is about spending quality time with your loved ones, being heedful and thankful for all our God-given blessings. So be kind to one another *and yourself* by tactfully managing your expectations.

Establishing connections with Allah ﷾ like this through our social interactions will help nourish our relationships with barakah, and will help purify our characters beyond Ramadan, insha'Allah.

The key question is: what are we waiting for?

Use the month of Sha'ban to implement beautiful values of extra God-consciousness (taqwa), kindness, humility, respect and generosity. Even if there is one thing you can positively implement in somebody else's life, it's a win—for them *and* for you.

Remember, we don't know how long we have in this world, so don't delay what you can do today for a tomorrow that you may never reach.

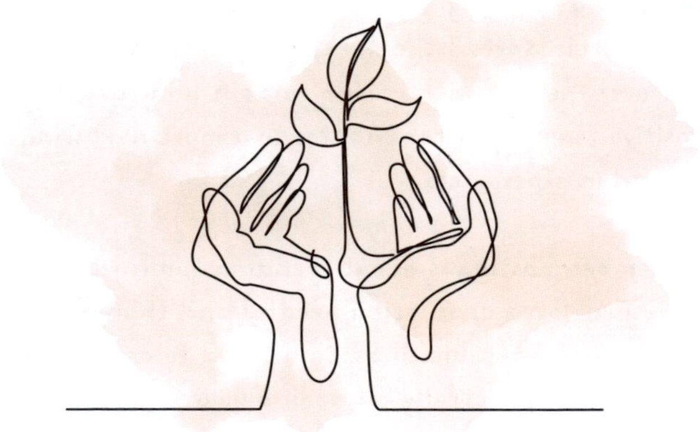

- I pray that Allah ﷾ allows us to start the month of Sha'ban with good and sincere intentions. I pray that He allows us to seek forgiveness and rebuild our relationships with our brothers and sisters leading up to Ramadan. I pray that He instils in each of us the drive to grow into better versions of ourselves.

- I pray that we are able to make the most of the blessed month of Sha'ban in order to successfully prepare our mind, body and soul for a transformative Ramadan, maximising the blessings of this month and the next. I pray that Allah ﷾ gives us the wisdom to plan effectively for success, exercise discipline and reflect on our actions. I pray that He gives us the wisdom to disconnect from the things that would weaken our souls, and guide us to connect with the beautiful aspects of our deen that will help us grow strong roots from within. As of today, I pray that we pour into the month of Sha'ban the respect that it is owed, and that we all prepare ourselves for a truly fulfilling and elevating Ramadan.

Ameen

Du'as for Sha'ban

We can start to use some time in Sha'ban to normalise supplication to Allah ﷻ. Know that He is near to us, hears us and knows us better than we know ourselves.

He knows that we are not perfect and nor does He expect us to be. He is our glorious Maker, and only He knows all the answers and solutions to our needs.

❀ A supplication is a genuine honest, open call and prayer to your Lord. What things would you like to share with Allah ﷻ, and what support/guidance/mercy would you like from Him?

- Open your hands in prayer as the first step of opening yourself up to Him. There are no secrets between you and Him. You can raise your hands, or you could choose to speak to Him in sujood (prostration), where you might feel the closest to Him—do whatever makes you feel most comfortable and present.

- Be sincere and ask for whatever is in your heart, both in times of ease as well as hardship—even if you don't know what you want or how you're feeling in the moment, thanking Allah ﷻ for His countless blessings and asking Allah ﷻ to forgive any of your misgivings is a good place to start.

- He is the Provider and Protector of all things; have hope in His mercy.

- Whatever you are asking for will most likely change from day to day based on how you are feeling, what you need help with, and what your goals are.

- Normalise this reserved, private 'talk' with your Lord in the day and choose a time you prefer to do this best. Some people prefer to start their day with this after their Fajr salah, while others prefer to do it in small chunks after each salah, or as a way to comfort themselves before they sleep. Start building a habit of supplication at least once in your day and zone out this 'quality time' with Allah ﷻ. You are never truly alone.

We find ourselves spending so much time chasing the world, when, in fact, we should be seeking the closeness, love and comfort of our Lord's attention.

So let's start now.

Let's become well versed in speaking with our Maker as opposed to just speaking to Him.

Reflecting our heart in our words

Here are some useful du'as you can refer to in your supplication—choose whichever one seems most appropriate to your feelings for that day.

The key is not in the quantity of du'as, but the **quality** - your meaning, feeling and intention behind the words. If you feel your du'as often sound and feel automatic, but not truly sincere, use the month of Sha'ban to start afresh by handpicking what you want to say to Allah ﷻ, and reflect on the meaning of, and your intention behind, the words you are using.

For example, when you are reciting:

سُبْحَانَ اللهِ

SubḥānAllāh

after your salah, which is highly recommended, are you reading it thirty-three times while thinking of the reward? Are you in the habit of reciting these really quickly, and before you know it, you've recited it without actually internalising it? Are you rushing off your prayer mat as you don't have time to read it thirty-three times?

Instead of counting, as you recite SubhanAllah, think of any of the following meanings that this phrase encompasses:

- Allah is Perfect
- Allah is the most Glorious
- How beautiful Allah's creation is, the birds that fly, the night and day, how stunning the plants and colours are
- How Allah has given us so much, the blessings we can't begin to count

As you recite SubhanAllah each time, think of what aspect of this phrase you would like to celebrate and honour about your Lord. Reciting this way makes us so much more appreciative of Allah ﷻ, and His countless blessings. Use this method of interpretation and apply it to whatever remembrance you are reciting.

Even if you are pressed for time, you can recite just a few of the shortest supplications or phrases, pressing the tips of your fingers as you consider their meaning.

Here are some other useful, short phrases you should make a habit of reciting either to open your supplication, or to close it:

ٱلْحَمْدُ لِلَّهِ

Alḥamdulillāh

All praise is due to Allah

لَا إِلَٰهَ إِلَّا ٱللَّهُ

Lā ilāha illallāh

There is none worthy of worship except Allah

اللّٰهُ أَكْبَر

Allāhu Akbar

Allah is Greater

أَسْتَغْفِرُ اللّٰهَ

Astaghfirullāh

I seek Allah's forgiveness

لَا حَوْلَ وَلَا قُوَّةَ إِلَّا بِٱللّٰهِ

Lā ḥawla wa lā quwwata illā billāh

There is no power or might except (by) Allah

Here are some short but beautiful du'as that are suitable for this phase of our growth:

يَا مُقَلِّبَ الْقُلُوبِ ثَبِّتْ قَلْبِي عَلَى دِينِكَ

Ya muqallibal qulūb, thabbit qalbī 'alā dīnik

O Turner of the hearts, make my heart firm on Your religion.

(Tirmidhi)

يَا مُصَرِّفَ الْقُلُوبِ صَرِّفْ قُلُوبَنَا عَلَى طَاعَتِكَ

Ya muṣarrifal qulūb, ṣarrif qulūbanā 'alā ṭā'atika

O director of hearts, direct my heart to your good deeds.

(Muslim)

Remember to supplicate for everyone—this is a beautiful du'a that encompasses this:

رَبِّ ٱجْعَلْنِى مُقِيمَ ٱلصَّلَوٰةِ وَمِن ذُرِّيَّتِى ۚ رَبَّنَا
وَتَقَبَّلْ دُعَآءِ رَبَّنَا ٱغْفِرْ لِى وَلِوَٰلِدَىَّ وَلِلْمُؤْمِنِينَ
يَوْمَ يَقُومُ ٱلْحِسَابُ

Rabbij 'alnī muqīmaṣ ṣalāti wa min dhurriyyatī. Rabbanā wa taqabbal du'ā. Rabbanagh fir lī waliwalidayya wa lil muminīna yawma yaqūmul ḥisāb

Lord, grant that I and my offspring may keep up the prayer. Our Lord, accept my request. Our Lord, forgive me, my parents and the believers on the Day of Reckoning.

(Ibrahim, 14:40-41)

As we pray to Allah ﷾, we pray for our beloved Prophet ﷺ as commanded to us in the Qur'an:

God and His angels bless the Prophet – so, you who believe, bless him too and give him greetings of peace.
(Al-Ahzab, 33:56)

We can use these words:

اللَّهُمَّ صَلِّ وَسَلِّمْ عَلَى نَبِيِّنَا مُحَمَّدٍ

Allāhumma ṣalli wa sallim ʿalā nabiyyinā Muḥammadin

O Allah, we ask for your peace and blessings upon our Prophet Muhammad ﷺ

Ramadan–
A time for growth

The blessed days and nights have arrived. Ramadan is here! If you've not had time to prepare for your spiritual growth as well as you wanted to, it is not too late to start now.

It was narrated by Abu Huraira ﵁ that the Prophet Muhammad ﷺ said:
"When the month of Ramadan starts, the gates of heaven are opened and the gates of Hell are closed and the devils are chained." (Bukhari)

This is therefore the month to truly nurture your soul and strengthen your connection with Allah ﷻ. Don't look back—use this month to keep moving towards growth.

Mindfulness

You who believe, fasting is prescribed for you, as it was prescribed for those before you, so that you may be mindful of God (Al-Baqarah, 2:183)

The purpose of fasting, as emphasised in this verse, is primarily to help us rewire our minds to God-consciousness, where we are more mindful of Allah ﷻ in everything that we do.

The following sections will look at how we can best achieve this.

Suhoor (pre-dawn meal)

One of the best ways to practise mindfulness is to start by improving our diligence towards suhoor. Many consider the beginning of the fast the most challenging, where our deepest slumber is broken. By the middle of the month, when that new feeling of Ramadan adrenalin is wearing off, getting up for and preparing suhoor becomes increasingly difficult. Some of us may be living or fasting independently, and may struggle to get up at all.

It is important that we rise for suhoor before Fajr to complete the tradition of our beloved Prophet ﷺ. This does require personal discipline and some adjustment, but this is where our growth lies, and it is also what distinguishes us from people of the earlier scriptures.

There are some helpful strategies, though, that we can use to make suhoor time more manageable and beneficial for the rest of the day:

- If you have trouble waking up for suhoor, plan to go to sleep immediately after your completing your Tarawih prayers—stay away from distractions before sleeping, such as staying at the masjid for a chat, scrolling through your phone, checking WhatsApp messages or social media posts.

- Before you close your eyes, make a sincere intention to wake up for Fajr, and pray Allah ﷻ makes it easier for you to rise, in order for you to fulfil the sunnah of the Prophet ﷺ—who is better to ask for help with this than Allah ﷻ?

- After making your intention, have a firm belief that you will be getting up.

- Set three consecutive alarms with loud buzzers, and put your alarms a little further away from you, so that you have to get up to turn them off.

- Drink plenty of water before sleeping; this way, you will naturally wake up to go to the bathroom.

- If you are living with family or friends who are fasting, can you support each other in getting up? Family members can help wake each other.

- If you are living or doing suhoor on your own and struggle to wake up, could you arrange for a reliable family member or friend to call you at that time? Keep your ringtone on a loud volume and under your pillow, so that you are able to hear their call when sleeping. This can make those really early starts feel more manageable, and turn the quiet hours into more of a shared experience.

- If you struggle to stay awake during suhoor, decide on a meal before sleeping, and ideally have what you need out ready so that you don't spend too much time looking for things.

- Make sure that what you eat will fill you with energy for the day, and drink plenty of water to keep you hydrated.

❧ If you are not a fan of heavy meals so early in the morning, following the sunnah of having dates and water will also suffice. If you genuinely do not like dates, then you could replace this with bananas.

❧ After eating your meal, renew your intention to fast, thanking Allah ﷻ for His provision (rizq), and make a du'a for a productive day of fasting where you can be the best version of yourself.

وَبِصَوْمِ غَدٍ نَّوَيْتُ مِنْ شَهْرِ رَمَضَانَ

Wa biṣawmi ghadin nawaytu min shahri Ramaḍān

I intend to keep the fast for tomorrow in the month of Ramadan. (Abu Dawud)

Despite all your best efforts, if for whatever reason you do not manage to wake up for suhoor, then know that it's still valid for you to fast if you made the intention before sleeping. This is Allah's Mercy.

It is also worth bearing in mind, though, that just as Allah ﷻ sees when we do make the effort and get up for Fajr or suhoor, He also sees when we are not making a conscious effort to be diligent, thereby missing the opportunity to connect with our Lord before the day begins.

Wudu

Ramadan is the perfect month to start considering how mindful we are about the way we purify our bodies.

Do you find that you rush your wudu, so that you can quickly get it over and done with? Do you try to keep your wudu for as long as possible, so you don't have to renew it for the next prayer? Or do you start off by making a sincere intention to complete your wudu, and do this obligatory purification mindfully before every prayer?

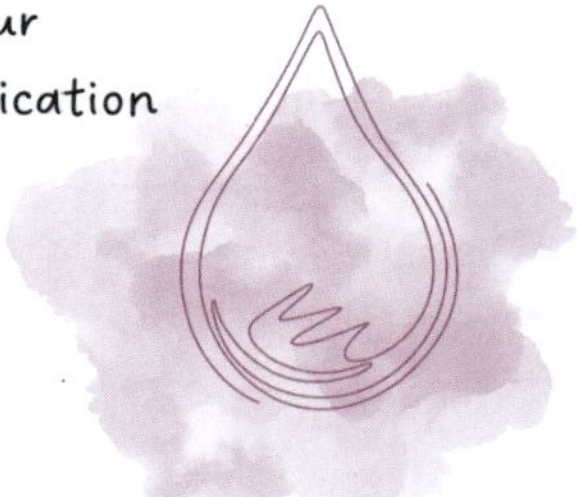

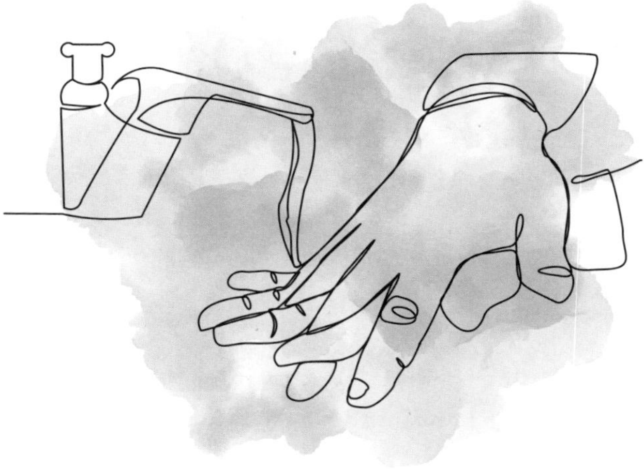

To help us think of wudu as an act of worship in itself, it may help to think about this first:

- Who are you about to stand in front of in devotion to pray? What does this mean?
- When you prepare for an important meeting, do you rush to get ready at the very last minute, or do you take your time to present yourself well?
- Why do we need to perform ablution?

We should think more carefully about **why** we are purifying our body with wudu, and the benefit that it brings to our day and in our prayer.

Performing ablution is a means of forgiveness of sins.

'Uthman ibn 'Affan narrated that Allah's Messenger said: *"Whoever does wudu and does wudu well, his sins come out of his body, even from beneath his nails."* (Ahmad)

- As we wash our hands, our sins fall off. Whatever we did with our hands and fingers, that was sinful, has been washed away.
- As we rinse our mouth, our sins are cleansed. Whatever we may have said that was displeasing, Allah washed it all away.
- As we wash our face, wipe over our heads and wash our ears, our sins are washed away. The sins we may have done with our eyes in what we were watching, and the sins of what we were listening to or overheard, are all washed away.
- Finally, as we wash our feet, our sins of where we walked towards are all washed away too.

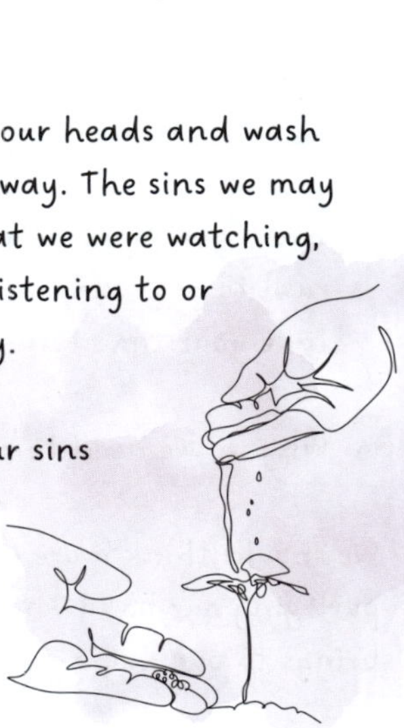

So next time, even when your ablution is valid and the time for prayer has come, stop and walk to the bathroom to renew it. Don't regard wudu as a ritual task or as a burden for it is a blessing beyond our understanding.

After completing wudu, 'Umar ibn al-Khattab رضي الله عنه narrated that the Messenger of Allah ﷺ said: *"Whoever performs ablution, then on completing it says,*

أَشْهَدُ أَنْ لَا إِلَهَ إِلَّا اللَّهُ وَ أَشْهَدُ أَنَّ مُحَمَّدًا عَبْدُهُ وَرَسُولُهُ

Ashhadu an lā ilahā illallāh, wa ashhadu anna Muḥammadan 'abduhū wa rasūluhū

I bear witness that none has the right to be worshipped but Allah, and I bear witness that Muhammad is His servant and His Messenger

eight gates of Paradise will be opened to him and he may enter through whichever one he wants."

(Nasa'i)

Salah

Ramadan is not solely about giving up food, drink and desires. It's essentially about connecting (or in many cases, reconnecting) with Allah ﷻ, and what better way to engage with Him than to stand up and pray salah?

What are the benefits of praying?

Just like Ramadan, prayer is a key pillar and thus at the heart of everything. In daily salah, you will find true inner peace and a strong sense of purpose, as the Qur'an tells us:

> So [Prophet] be patient with what they say - celebrate the praise of your Lord, before the rising and setting of the sun, celebrate His praise during the night, and at the beginning and end of the day, so that you may find contentment. (Ta-Ha, 20:130)

> Order your people to pray, and pray steadfastly yourself. We are not asking you to give Us provision; We provide for you, and the rewards of the Hereafter belong to the devout. (Ta-Ha, 20:132)

Salah keeps us rooted in our faith and submission to Allah ﷾. The more you pray, the more you ask for Allah's ﷾ help, the more perspective you get on your purpose in this world.

Think of salah as an anchor that keeps us from straying from the right path, and a moral compass that navigates us to our ultimate, desired destination. The more regular your prayers are, the more God-conscious and mindful you will be of your actions and speech.

Witness how your good deeds blossom from you as a result of salah.

Allah ﷻ reminds us in the Qur'an:

> [Prophet], recite what has been revealed to you of the Scripture; keep up the prayer: prayer restrains outrageous and unacceptable behaviour. Remembering God is greater: God knows everything you are doing. (Al-'Ankabut, 29:45)

Now that we have been reminded of the powerful impact of salah, it follows that this should be central to our growth journey.

Make this a non-negotiable target for yourself.

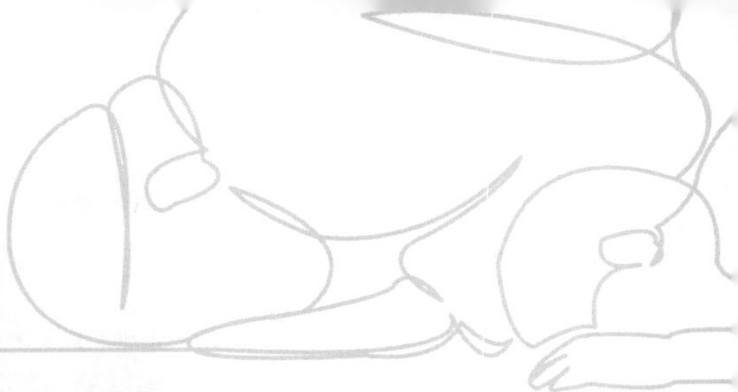

Prioritise and work around prayer. Just as a plant seeks out the light for its survival, we should be using salah to connect with Allah ﷻ and strengthen our soul. Islam offers us the beautiful gift of being able to connect with our Lord at least five specific times in a day, every day.

Taking the time out to perform wudu, speaking honestly about what is in our hearts to our Lord, and praising and reflecting on our Lord's amazing generosity offers us the solace, humbleness and strength to be able to carry on with our day with grace, regardless of the challenges we might face in the world. It is therefore essential for us that we pause our day for the sustenance of salah in order activate the growth that happens in between them.

How can we be more consistent with our salah?

Here are some useful tips:

- Set the prayer times on your phone's calendar. You can always put these on silent or vibration mode, so that you can see the notifications, without causing disruption. Having an alarm at the start of the prayer time and a second to signal the latest time you can pray would be useful, if it's difficult for you to pray on time while working.

- It helps to start a culture at home of reminding each other of prayer time, as a way of guiding each other to success. Even asking 'Did you read Maghrib?' sets the expectation for a more consistent salah at home. Without these conversations, it can become difficult especially for those who lack motivation or get easily distracted to commit to their salah journey.

- Ask your local mosque for their salah calendar (many provide one), and put this up on your fridge, or somewhere very visible and accessible for you, so that you can see it every day.

- If you are working or studying, then try and have your breaks around prayer time, if you are able to, or integrate your prayer into your breaks. If you work or study with a Muslim, motivate and remind each other about the salah times, being conscious of the sincere intentions you made at the start of Ramadan.

- Making a sincere intention is often the first step to getting things done! Did you make a sincere intention to pray your salah? Did you make du'a to your Lord to help you become more consistent and timely with your salah? NEVER underestimate the power of earnest intention and du'a—this is the first step to mindful practice. And with these requests comes barakah.

Insha'Allah, with perseverance and determination, working your day around your salah will begin to feel more organic for you. The key is to not give up on your salah journey, even if you do forget to pray one. Keep trying, for the sake of Allah ﷻ.

Do you struggle to get up for Fajr?

Getting up for Fajr can feel like a challenge for many, just as suhoor can feel difficult. However, Ramadan is an ideal time to develop this beneficial habit.

Ask yourself this: imagine if you had everything you could ever dream of in this world. What would that look like?

Well, it is remarkable when we remind ourselves that:

> *The two rak'ah before the dawn (Fajr) prayer are better than this world and all it contains.*
> (Riyad as-Salihin)

What could we, therefore, do to help us wake up for such a blessed Fajr salah? You can refer back the suhoor section for tips on how to wake up.

It helps to know that you are being witnessed and your efforts are being noticed by Allah ﷻ, who is Ar-Raqeeb—The Watchful, The Witness—and the angels are stationed behind you as you pray:

> Abu Huraira ؓ narrated that the Prophet ﷺ said: *"Angels take turns around you, some at night and some by day, and all of them assemble together at the time of the Fajr and 'Asr prayers."* (Bukhari)

This is a great motivator for completing salah and praying it **mindfully**.

Developing a habit of reading Fajr in Ramadan feels a little easier when you are waking up for suhoor. Instead of rushing back to bed after making your intention to fast, complete your wudu instead, and pray your Fajr salah. It's only going to take an extra few minutes of devotion, and the rewards for this will be innumerable, insha'Allah.

Begin implementing the habit of Fajr prayer while it feels more natural to do so during Ramadan, so that you find the practice easier to sustain beyond it.

Are you praying, but struggling to focus?

While we stand up with the best intentions to pray, and our words and limbs demonstrate our submission to and connection with our Lord, we sometimes find that our **heart** is not always connected to those actions. Our minds start to wander, and our attention to Allah ﷻ—which should be undivided—becomes distracted by our thoughts about worldly matters. Before you know it, the prayer has finished and you don't truly know what you've read.

So what can we do to help increase concentration during our salah?

- Pick a place where you feel calm in terms of your surroundings. Sometimes, if your surroundings are cluttered, your mind feels the same way too.

- Turn off any noise that may disturb you and put your phone on silent.

- Think about Whom you are standing in front of, Whom you are praising and seeking help from.

- Get yourself in the zone for prayer a few minutes before. If you have a lot on your plate one day, and your mind feels busy with thoughts, take a deep breath, sit on your prayer mat and make a few supplications before you pray. This will help quieten your mind, especially if you internalise the supplications you are reciting and focus on their meaning nice and slowly.

- It is recommended that we refresh ourselves on the meaning of the recitations in our salah in our native language, and remember these meanings as we recite them. Once you see salah as a conversation with Allah ﷻ, and not a mindless recitation or tick-box exercise, your concentration in salah will blossom.

- Reciting slowly and deliberately helps bring back the focus if the mind begins to wander. It helps zone out the thoughts and bring you back into prayer.

- If you find that your mind starts to stray during the prayer, take a deep breath and pause, before continuing or reciting the words again.

You may have days where you're not feeling motivated; you're struggling with your salah, and want to give up... Go to your prayer mat and pray anyway. Turn up. It's the absolute least we can do for our Maker.

Seek help with steadfastness and prayer - though this is hard indeed for anyone but the humble

(Al-Baqarah, 2:45)

Allah ﷻ knows what is in our hearts, so ask for help. Even if it feels awkward or difficult to put it into words.

The purpose of connecting with Allah ﷾ is not to rush through our prayers and get them over and done with as quickly as possible. It's about devoting yourself in prayer to Allah ﷾ with a sense of meaning. It's about reciting mindfully, not mindlessly; paying attention as opposed to being heedless; being thankful and being present, despite our imperfections.

While Allah is indeed our Judge, He is not judgemental when He knows someone is genuinely trying, regardless of their struggles.

For those that are consistent with praying, how can you enhance your prayer even more in Ramadan?

If you already have developed good habits and are praying five times a day, you could exert yourself by adding a few voluntary prayers. As motivation, Allah ﷻ tells us in the Qur'an:

> **And during the night, wake up and pray, as an extra offering of your own, so that your Lord may raise you to a [highly] praised status.** (Al-Isra, 17:79)

These voluntary prayers are also referring to the Tahajjud prayers—the time after 'Isha prayer and before Fajr prayer, when angels descend from heaven on Allah's ﷻ command to take our du'as.

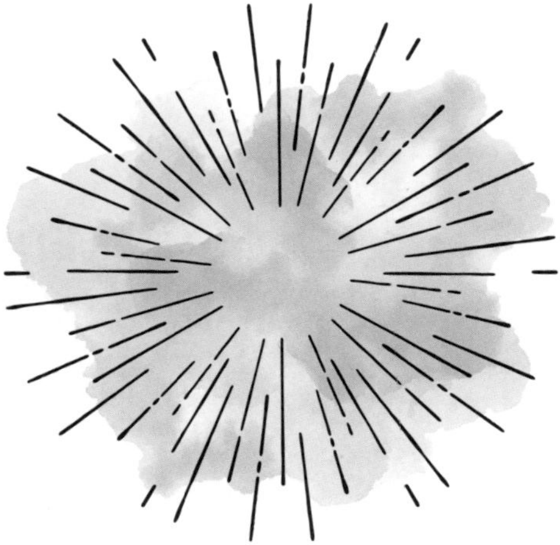

Abu Huraira ﷺ narrated that the Prophet ﷺ said: When it is the last third of the night, our Lord, the Blessed, the Superior, descends every night to the heaven of the world and says, *"Is there anyone who invokes Me (demand anything from Me), that I may respond to his invocation; Is there anyone who asks Me for something that I may give (it to) him; Is there anyone who asks My forgiveness that I may forgive him?"* (Bukhari)

With this in mind, if you are getting up for suhoor, perhaps you could motivate yourself to get up a little earlier to take advantage of the blessed time of Tahajjud.

Other ways to take your basic salah practice to the next level would be to:

- Renew your ablution for each prayer, even though it still might be valid. Think of your sins being washed away as you do this.

- Pray promptly at the start of the time window—you could put a reminder on your phone ten minutes before the start time, just like we do for other important meetings or events that we do not want to be late for.

- Read voluntary prayers in addition to Tahajjud, such as Ishraq after sunrise.

- Dedicate extra time by incorporating more supplications, especially in your prostration when we are the closest to Allah سبحانه وتعالى.

Qur'an

It was in the month of Ramadan that the Qur'an was revealed as guidance for mankind, clear messages giving guidance and distinguishing between right and wrong. (Al-Baqarah, 2:185)

Many of us know this and have the best of intentions to read the Qur'an this month. But how does one find time to zone out from studying, doing exams, working, running the family home, looking after children for those with families, and helping parents? The list of responsibilities sometimes feels endless. How are we going to find time to read all of the Qur'an in thirty days? For sisters, even less than thirty days, if you are menstruating.

If you find yourself struggling to juggle everything and finish reading the whole Qur'an, consider this:

- Isn't it better to recite the Qur'an a little at a time, but consistently, and with meaning and clarity, than to rush to recite the whole Qur'an in Ramadan, exhausting yourself as a result? The latter often results in people not wanting to read the Qur'an for the rest of the year as a consequence. Which experience sounds more purposeful and connected to Allah ﷻ?

- Pace yourself and read what you can comfortably manage. The easiest way to develop a habit is to start off small.

To make this easier, let's break this down with some practical examples:

- Is there something that you do each day at a specific time where you could read the Qur'an within that time? For example, could you read for a few minutes in the morning when you are on your way to school or work?

- Often in Ramadan, many of us opt to miss breaks or lunches, so that we can finish early. Whilst this is great, it would also be good to have a little break during the day where you could engage with the Qur'an to truly give yourself a break from the pressures of work and studying—the words of Allah سبحانه وتعالى will recharge, ground and recentre you when you might feel stretched.

- If you normally scroll through your phone before bed, could you dedicate these five minutes to Qur'an time instead during Ramadan?

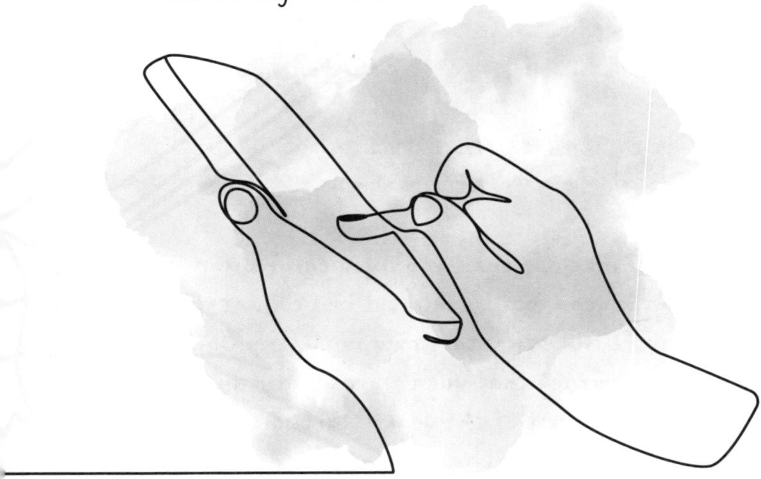

- If you are a morning person, could you stay on the prayer mat after Fajr and read at least one page of the Qur'an?

Dedicating a few minutes in your entire day to the Holy Qur'an sounds far more manageable now, doesn't it? Making a conscious effort to embed your connection with Allah ﷻ like this throughout your day, around your schedule (ideally at the very beginning and end of your day), feels more natural. Set yourself a realistic goal, no matter how small. You might think to yourself that five minutes is not very much at all, and that you can do more.

My advice is, whatever target you set yourself, half it to start off with. If you end up doing more, that's great.

The key is not to set a target you are going to struggle with and then end up giving up altogether.

However much of the Qur'an you can read in Ramadan is good, but wouldn't it be brilliant if Ramadan felt like the start of a long-term Qur'an journey—a journey that you can easily continue throughout the rest of the year? Start small and be consistent, and if you end up reading more because you want to, then that's a special bonus.

Why should we read and recite the Qur'an? What effect will this have on us?

We believe and declare our faith as Muslims; however, do we really know what Allah's ﷻ beneficial messages and instructions for our own success are?

The Qur'an is our book of guidance—a means of soothing our heart, nourishing our soul and purifying our actions in this world, in preparation for the next. Everything we need to know is all in the Qur'an, so make this your first point of reference to seek knowledge about what it means to be a good Muslim. Allah ﷻ is the Most Loving and Most Merciful. He doesn't expect us to second-guess fundamental aspects of our way of life. He's given us the manual for success, and guidance to bring us closer to Him. So let's use this guidance to help us strive for success.

There are so many stories in the Qur'an that still relate to us today. Some of the stories will relate to your personal situation more than others; there is something in the Qur'an for everyone, regardless of your life journey, age, level of faith and worldly experience. Remember that any form of engagement with the Qur'an is a form of worship. So while running errands, or when on your way to school or work, listen to the recitation of the Qur'an in Arabic and/or a clear translation. Sisters—you can do this even when menstruating due to the lack of physical touch.

Reading, reflecting or listening to the Qur'an makes us feel more spiritually connected with our Lord when we remember that its unchanged, sacred words have been revealed first and foremost directly by Him, our Maker. The feeling of not having recited the Qur'an for a while is a distinct one, like the pang of not hearing the voice of one who loves us most for some time. So make the effort to connect; carve out this much-needed time in your day for the Holy Qur'an in either physical or digital form, so that you are gifted with the feeling of unmatched, inner peace.

From my personal experience, once you start reading the Qur'an, and truly getting to know it, you will naturally want to read and reflect more as time goes on. It will start to make a home in your heart ❦

Arabic or English?

How can the Qur'an touch your heart if you don't know what you are reading?

If Arabic is not your first language, don't feel guilty about reading a translation of the Qur'an in your own native language. If you struggle to read Arabic, don't let that demotivate you from engaging with the Qur'an. Allah ﷻ is the Creator of all speech, so don't feel guilty in trying to understand His words in a language that you better understand.

In addition to reading translations, you can read or listen to commentaries/explanations and reflect upon them. Don't compare yourself to others; do whatever you can do best, for the key is to connect with the Message.

Keep a translation of the Qur'an somewhere respectful where you can always see it, pick it up and read it during the day. Sometimes you may only read a page or two, sometimes you might start reading, and not want to put it down. Keep it close to you, so that it remains clean with your touch, insha'Allah, as opposed to collecting dust from neglect.

This should not replace our effort to improve our reading and understanding of the Qur'an in Arabic; it serves to aid our understanding and connection to Allah ﷻ.

The Prophet ﷺ was asked, *"What deeds are loved most by Allah?" He said, "The most regular constant deeds even though they may be few." He added, "Don't take upon yourselves, except the deeds which are within your ability."* (Bukhari)

Hands

As well as our speech and attitudes, another aspect of us that requires God-consciousness is our hands. Our hands help demonstrate our mental well-being, feelings for and attitudes towards others, and are a powerful medium for self-control.

Reflect on how God-conscious we could be with our hands in a literal and figurative sense:

- Do we use the hands that our Lord created to carry out actions that would displease our Maker? Or do we strive to use our hands to perform good deeds that would please Him?

- How often do we raise our hands in supplication to the Most High? Do we pour our words into our cupped hands during supplication?

- How often do we use our hands to pray for others, as well as ourselves?

- How often do we guide and support people with our hands?

- How often do we hold the hands of the ill and elderly?

- Have we ever used our hands roughly, in anger or impatience? If we are prone to this, could we try tightening our fists in a ball and clench and unclench them, while taking long, slow breaths to avoid us using our hands aggressively?

- How do we give respect and love to the Holy Qur'an when it is in our hands?

- How often after prayer do we use our fingers to do dhikr of Allah ﷻ? How often do we use prayer beads (tasbeeh) and do dhikr in Ramadan?

- Do we use our hands to donate to the poor and needy, charities and institutions that will help our Ummah?

- Are we mindful of the specific type of words we type and send to others on our devices?

- Are we conscious of the types of things we search for on the internet, knowing that God is All-Seeing and All-Knowing?
- Do we try to filter what we 'like', who we 'follow' and be conscious of what we share with others on social media, so that we do not lead ourselves and others to sin?
- Are we God-conscious of what we choose to play on TV or on our devices?

And we can extend those reflections to all our body parts:

> **On the Day [of Judgement] when their tongues, their hands, and their legs or feet will bear witness against them as to what they used to do.**
> (An-Nur, 24:24)

Speech

Mindfulness in speech is a key attribute of a believer.

Abu Huraira ﵁ narrated that the Prophet ﷺ said: *"Whoever does not give up forged speech and evil actions, Allah is not in need of his leaving his food and drink."* (Bukhari)

Think about how we are using our tongue:

- Could you glorify and speak to your Lord for five quiet minutes after each Fard prayer?

- Be careful that your speech does not lead to talking about others in a negative light. Prevent yourself from backbiting as most people will enter the Fire because of this reason. It is very tempting in social gatherings to discuss people and their affairs. How can we limit this type of people-focused talk so that our conversation is full of goodness and piety in these sacred months, and beyond?

- Avoid negative talk of others at all costs. This includes saying something about someone that they would not like, even if what you are saying is true.

- Use your tongue to respect and defend others, especially when you know they are not present in the conversation. This links back to the importance of giving people the benefit of the doubt. It's easy to go with the flow and agree with the opinions of others to keep the peace; however, stop to think if what they are saying is fair and just. Think and speak mindfully, not mindlessly. Defend others in their absence as you would like to be defended in yours.

- If a discussion arises about a person, ask yourself whether what is being shared about them with you, and *how* it is being said, is pleasing to Allah سبحانه وتعالى. Act accordingly. Don't respond in anger or superiority. Be gentle and respectful in your response, for we are all a work in progress, when steering the conversation in a new direction.

**Mindful speech is not limited to Muslims;
it extends to everyone regardless of faith or creed.**

With practice and discipline, we can become better and better at moderating our own words for the benefit of ourselves and others. Our beloved Prophet Muhammad ﷺ was renowned for his selective and purposeful speech. He spoke with the best of manners to everyone—his children, wives, family, Companions and other Muslims and non-Muslims in society. He never spoke out of turn to those who spoke disrespectfully to him, never spoke excessively (for the sake of speaking), and was known for his beautifully disciplined speech. Let's strive to be so considerate with our language during Ramadan that it becomes second nature to us beyond it, insha'Allah.

In addition to this, at the start of the fasting day, make a sincere intention for kind, respectful, unhypocritical speech. At the end of your fasting day, ask for Allah's ﷾ forgiveness in case you were not careful with your speech, and reflect on how you could better approach a conversation next time, to encourage personal growth.

Respect for others

In addition to being mindful of the words you share with others, it is also important to be considerate and empathetic towards those who you are preparing meals for you.

Self-restraint applies to everything that we do during the month of Ramadan, from the amount and type of food we consume, to our expectations of others.

It's time to further develop the healthier attitude towards our consumption that we began reflecting on in Sha'ban.

If you are invited to open your fast, remind yourself of this:

> Abu Huraira ﷺ narrated that the Prophet ﷺ said: *"I shall accept the invitation even if I were invited to a meal of a sheep's trotter, and I shall accept the gift even if it were an arm or a trotter of a sheep."* (Bukhari)

If someone kindly offers to open your fast, show your thanks with humility and kindness, for we are not entitled to these offerings; this is a blessing from Allah ﷻ, and we should therefore strive to not take for granted people's generosity. If you accept the kind offer, remember to manage your expectations: don't expect a variety of different dishes, or allow yourself to feel disappointed if there were not enough starters, mains or desserts of your liking. Always try to put yourself in your host's shoes. They would have had an extremely busy day during Ramadan, in addition to preparation and cooking for iftar. Additionally, they would have been fasting themselves. Unless you have specific dietary requirements due to unavoidable circumstances (which hopefully you will have pre-advised your host about), refrain from being picky.

Here are just a few acts of consideration that we could practise:

- Before attending, have you offered to help in any way? Could you offer to bring one dish to provide some relief to your host's preparations?

- Embrace the spirit of Ramadan, be humble and grateful for even the simplest of offerings. As you collectively sit down to open your fast, do you display sincere appreciation of their efforts by supplicating for the host?

- When you have finished your meal, don't forget to thank the host in earnest for their generosity, and offer your help with the clearing up—your host has already spent a lot of time preparing their meal; so having to clean up themselves just before their night prayers can become very tiring. Helping each other out to clean up before Tarawih prayer would be much more considerate, and is another way of showing your appreciation for the host's efforts.

- Always be mindful not to overstay your welcome. Whilst you may be having a great time, each of you in the household will want to pray and get some rest, so that you are ready for the next day.

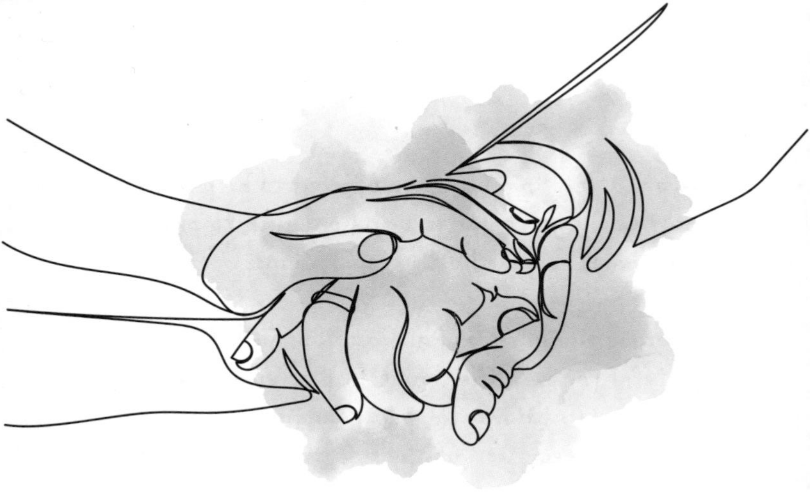

We have explored some important host and guest etiquettes at length here; but we must use these suggestions to remind ourselves of the constant figures in our lives who check up on us and look after us every day. During Ramadan and beyond, why don't we therefore ensure we also extend these etiquettes of appreciation and respect to the people in our lives who deserve it the most?

Think about how you can show your appreciation to these people this Ramadan.
Honour them first and foremost in your prayers.

The Mosque

Abu Huraira ﷺ narrated that Allah's Messenger ﷺ used to urge people to perform optional Tarawih prayers at night during the month of Ramadan and said: *"Whosoever performs (optional Tarawih) prayers at night during the month of Ramadan, with faith and in the hope of receiving Allah's reward, will have his past sins forgiven."* (Riyad as-Salihin)

So where should we pray? In the mosque, or at home?

Men usually strive to pray in the mosque where and when possible. The rewards of praying in the mosque are well known.

Abu Huraira ﷺ narrated that Allah's Messenger ﷺ said: *"The reward of the prayer offered by a person in congregation is twenty five times greater than that of the prayer offered in one's house or in the market (alone). And this is because if he performs ablution and does it perfectly and then proceeds to the mosque with the sole intention of praying, then for every step he takes towards the mosque, he is upgraded one degree in reward and his one sin is taken off (crossed out) from his accounts (of deeds). When he offers his prayer, the angels keep on asking Allah's Blessings and Allah's forgiveness for him as long as he is (staying) at his musalla. They say, 'O Allah! Bestow Your blessings upon him, be Merciful and kind to him.' And one is regarded in prayer as long as one is waiting for the prayer."* (Bukhari)

What beautiful words of encouragement these are, that combine worship with a sense of community. Many brothers who have found a local mosque and have started to attend during Ramadan have said they have found much peace and solace there, with many wanting to continue attending after Ramadan.

But what about the women?

For women, attending the mosque is entirely optional, depending on their individual circumstances and if the local mosque has facilities. Some years, I have prayed Tarawih in the mosque and this does give a beautiful sense of community spirit in Ramadan. It's nice to listen to the recitation of the Qur'an and meet and interact with sisters. There is nothing wrong with women attending the mosque to pray.

Ibn 'Umar ﵁ narrated that the Prophet Muhammad ﷺ said: *"If your women ask permission to go to the mosque at night, allow them."* (Bukhari)

However, it is also a lovely experience to take your time and read at home at your own pace. The rush to get to the mosque after iftar can often be stressful, due the shorter timeframe between Maghrib and 'Isha prayers.

The following narration mentions the excellence of women praying at home, so we shouldn't view it as 'less' compared to praying at the mosque.

Ibn Masud ﵁ reported that the Prophet ﷺ said: *"It is more excellent for a woman to pray in her house than in her courtyard, and more excellent for her to pray in her private chamber than in her house."* (Abu Dawud)

I pray that Allah ﷻ allows us to focus our mind on things that will bring us closer to Him. I pray that He gives us the wisdom and maturity to be increasingly mindful and God-conscious of our actions during Ramadan, to the point that this becomes second nature to us. I pray that we are thoughtful in how we use our speech and our body to please Allah ﷻ. I pray that He washes all of our sins away as we perform wudu, and purifies our soul. I pray that He makes it easy for us to wake up for suhoor, and motivates us to observe the beautiful sunnahs of our Prophet Muhammed ﷺ. I pray that Allah ﷻ accepts all of our humble efforts, showers us with His Mercy even when we struggle to be perfect in our practices, and makes it easier for us to implement these strategies for self-development more consistently over time.

Ameen

The last ten nights

Laylat al-Qadr is more than a night of forgiveness,
It's a night of decree.
Think about what growth you want
to see in yourself this year
And begin to prune the past by praying for forgiveness.
Make way for a stronger you by praying for guidance.
Before you know it, you'll be flowering,
Thanks to the night of decree.

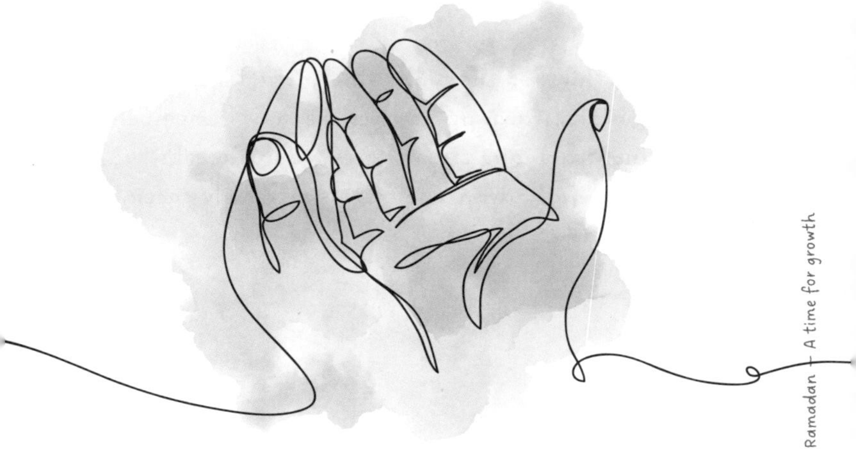

Why is Laylat al-Qadr a special night?

Laylat al-Qadr is known as the night of decree—a night of power, glory and blessing. It is believed to be the night when the Qur'an was sent down to mankind, during one of the last ten nights of Ramadan.

It is:

- A night when every matter of wisdom was made distinct.
- A night better than a thousand months, equivalent to eighty-three years.
- A night when the angels and the Spirit descend again and again.
- A night where there is peace until the break of dawn.

We often think of the night starting after we have prayed 'Isha and Tarawih; however, we must remember that the night actually starts after Maghrib. Let's therefore take full advantage of this extremely special phase of Ramadan.

What can we do on these nights?

To be able to move forward, we must be ready to move on from our past, so pray for forgiveness profusely, for the things you intended, did accidentally and in jest. Ask for forgiveness for all the big and little things that may come to mind, for while we have faith in Allah's ﷻ Compassion, we should not take His Kindness and Mercy for granted.

Aisha رضي الله عنها reported: I asked: *"O Messenger of Allah! If I realise Laylat al-Qadr (Night of Decree), what should I supplicate in it?"* He ﷺ replied that you should supplicate the following:

اللَّهُمَّ إِنَّكَ عَفُوٌّ تُحِبُّ الْعَفْوَ فَاعْفُ عَنِّي

Allahumma innaka 'afuwwun, tuḥibbul-'afwa, fa'fu 'annī

O Allah, You are Most Forgiving, and You love forgiveness; so forgive me. (Riyad as-Salihin)

Alongside this du'a, supplicate whole-heartedly with whatever you want to ask for.

There are many more ways we can make the most of these special nights. Do whatever you can in an effort to exert yourself a little more than you usually would. A few suggestions can be:

- Adding or increasing the amount of prayers, such as Tahajjud, night prayers, the sunnahs or nafl prayers.
- Reading, listening and reflecting on the Qur'an.
- Getting to know Allah ﷻ by studying and reciting His Beautiful Names.
- The male members of the community entering into i'tikaf (seclusion).
- Performing dhikr frequently throughout the days and nights.
- Sending blessings on the Prophet Muhammad ﷺ.
- Staying awake after Fajr till sunrise reading the Qur'an.

Keep searching for the night like it's your last. Only Allah ﷻ knows best which night this falls on as He is the Best of Planners. So take heed of every night in the last ten days as if it were the night of Laylat al-Qadr. Don't give up after one or two. Keep going with small and sustainable actions and persevere in your love for Allah ﷻ.

As much as we want to be able to commit to as many of these practices as possible, it can be difficult to stay up through the night when you have commitments early in the morning and during the day. For working people, it is therefore advisable to save some of your annual leave for the last few nights of Ramadan, so that you can participate in making the most of Laylat al-Qadr.

Equally, if you cannot get time off, and therefore are finding it challenging to observe these nights as diligently as you would like, don't worry. Don't let yourself feel deflated and compare yourself to others. Do the best that you possibly can in the hours you have around your work and family commitments. If your intentions are sincere and you are mindful in your acts of worship, you will be rewarded abundantly, insha'Allah.

You can only do the best that you can...

The responsibilities and daily commitments we have are still going to be there during Ramadan, so how can we possibly fit more time for worship in our day? We're already tired, still need to study, go to work, sort the children out, do the cleaning, washing, cooking, and shopping. The list is never ending. You may not be able to read lots of Qur'an; you may struggle to pray five times a day, with the addition of Tarawih prayers. Going to the mosque may be an impossibility due to your work patterns or distance from the mosque; or it could just be that you are too exhausted and then struggle to get up the next morning.

If you ever feel like this, take a big, deep breath. And be kind to yourself.

Spiritual blossoming can only take place when there is a balance in your inward nourishment of the soul and body, and outward exertion in worship. If there is a clear imbalance, and you are exerting outwards far more than taking care of mind and body, you will not be able to feel, enjoy or appreciate your strengthening connection with Allah ﷻ.

If you are feeling overwhelmed or a little out of your depth, consider that:

- Whatever responsibilities you are fulfilling, renew your intention behind them and hope for Allah's ﷻ reward—if you are working, you are still providing for your family. If you are maintaining the home, you are still helping to look after the family. Your sacrifices won't go unnoticed.

- Remember that Allah ﷻ loves the deeds that are carried out with sincerity, meaning and consistency, even if they are small. It's the **quality** of your worship that should be prioritised, not the quantity.

Allah ﷻ ultimately wants ease for His creation, not hardship. It is true that real, transformative growth occurs when we must step outside of our comfort zone. But embracing new challenges for personal development doesn't mean that you need to overburden yourself and suffer. Do not underestimate the power of balance and rest:

Abdullah ibn 'Amr ؓ reported that the Messenger of Allah ﷺ said: *"I have been informed that you stand for prayer the whole night and fast during the day. I said: I do that, whereupon he said: If you did that you in fact strained your eyes heavily and made yourself weak. There is a right of your eyes (upon you) and a right of yourself (upon you) and a right of your family (upon you). Stand for prayer and sleep. Observe fasts and break (them)."* (Muslim)

There are times where I've tried to stay up every night in the last ten nights and then fallen asleep half way through one of the odd nights. When this happens, I can't help but feel disappointed with myself. However, I've learnt to realise that my need to rest is a blessing from Allah ﷻ rather than a hindrance in my growth—a blessing in that I still fell asleep praising Allah ﷻ, and woke up thinking of praising Him. I recall the hadith above knowing that our body has a right upon us. We are not superhuman and need sleep to thrive.

We will truly blossom when our bodies and minds align. Take that shower; get a solid night's rest; wash your hair; trim your nails; dress yourself in fresh clean clothes; wear your favourite scent.

Worship of Allah is even more joyful when our body is given the due respect and attention it deserves.

Should we limit ourselves to asking for forgiveness alone?

Of course, we would not want to miss this blessed opportunity to pray for forgiveness of our past and present shortcomings. However, being a night of decree, we should also spend time in the last ten nights thinking about the year ahead and the time to come:

- How do you want to improve yourself this year? This could be in your habits, in your goals, in your relationships.
- How can you strive to become closer to Allah ﷻ?
- How can you strive to bring others closer to Allah ﷻ?
- How can you bring about positive, spiritual growth? This could be at home, at work, within your network of family and friends, or within your community.

These are all important conversations that you need to have with yourself. In recent years, I switched from making 'New Year' January resolutions (which I felt were goals with short term gains) to implementing more meaningful decisions and intentions in these nights that have shaped who I am today, and how I spend my time in more productive ways. The more effort you spend on connecting with the beautiful faith, and engaging with Allah's ﷻ revelation and the sunnahs of our beloved Prophet Muhammad ﷺ, you will begin to find answers to the questions above. You will naturally start to contemplate your purpose in this world and how that links to your Eternal journey. Whatever your goals are, remember to make sincere intentions, and persevere in your efforts—you will grow as you intended, insha'Allah.

What if I can't fast?

You may suffer from an illness where fasting will further deteriorate your health. You may have unexpected travel plans in the event of a family bereavement. You could be working long hours back-to-back, or tiring night shifts to provide for your family, which means you may not able to pray the night prayers in the mosque with other brothers. You may have had exams or deadlines, and therefore were not able to engage in a much worship as much as you would have liked.

Sisters, there may be circumstances where you have planned how you intend to spend your days and nights, and then menstruation comes along. In this case, try to do as much as you can before your menstruation time arrives, as you know this is inevitable.

Whatever the reason, it can leave you feeling a little left out with everyone who is fasting around you. What is the best way to cope with this?

Acknowledge that Allah ﷻ sees and knows your individual struggles, and He is Merciful. Know that you can only do what is within your means. If you feel you have no choice but to defer your fast, keep a record of this, and make it your responsibility to make up for it as soon as you are able to, if this is medically possible.

Remind yourself of this narration:

> Umar ibn al-Khattab ؓ reported that the Prophet ﷺ said: *"The reward of deeds depends upon the intentions and every person will get the reward according to what he has intended."* (Bukhari)

- We know our bodies have a right upon us. So menstruation, illness and injury that require medical treatment are all blessed exemptions in the month of Ramadan. This is Allah's ﷿ mercy.

- Since these conditions or experiences were ordained by our Lord, why do allow ourselves to suffer denial from their existence? These are not punishments or bouts of bad luck. These are God's will. If you make your sincere intentions, and something comes up that is beyond your control, don't despair. Have hope that Allah ﷿ will reward you with what you intended, despite the unexpected change of plans, and the reward may be more than you can imagine. Subhan'Allah.

- Allah ﷿ wants ease for us and not hardship. He tells us not to pray and fast when the body is experiencing severe challenges, and by doing so, we are obeying His command, which is an act of worship in itself.

Rather than becoming disheartened and focusing on what you can't do, which is counter-productive, focus instead on the positives: harness that feeling of self-consciousness that you may have when not being able to fast into carrying out other spiritual acts and deeds. You could actively engage in the following:

- Make an extra effort to exert yourself in charitable actions, such as feeding the poor, volunteering work.
- Busy your tongue with Allah's ﷻ remembrance.
- Supplicate for forgiveness.
- Listen to audios of the Qur'an or Islamic reminders reflect on the messages.
- If you are physically able to do, actively help others with opening their fasts, and be considerate and supportive to those around you who are fasting. Is there anything you could kindly do for them to relieve them of their home duties while they fast?
- Send blessings upon our beloved Prophet ﷺ in abundance.
- Use the extra time you feel you may have during this period to plan your goals in becoming closer

to Allah ﷻ, and make du'a for yourself, your loved ones, and the Ummah—those who are able to fast and who cannot—that their efforts, deeds and good intentions are accepted and rewarded greatly during the month of Ramadan.

Don't lose hope, and trust in The Divine. Have faith in the fact that Allah ﷻ is genuinely the best of planners. If your Ramadan plans have unexpectedly changed to something you had not desired, remember that there is good in this for you. While we do not take Allah's Mercy ﷻ for granted when making decisions, we should always have hope in His Compassion.

Acts of charity, big and small

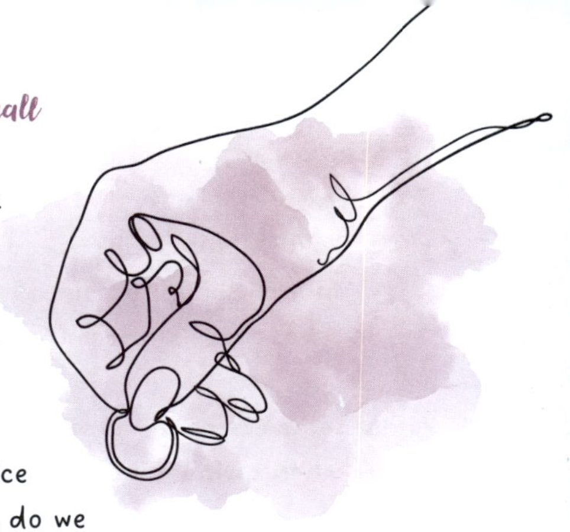

The month of Ramadan is a time where many Muslims donate money, food, water and clothes generously to those who are less fortunate than us – an essential practice in our religion. However, do we think carefully about **where** we donate to, and **why**? Do any of us automate our donations each month, not being as attentive as we should be about exactly what **kind** of support is being given to those who most need it, and **how** that charity will help them?

Keep your heart open to charity and your mind engaged with those suffering around the world. Think more carefully about the specific causes you want to donate to. Engage in research, and make more informed decisions about who and how you are helping, rather than giving compulsory charity (Zakat) and voluntary charity (Sadaqah) without engaging your heart to the cause. To help achieve this, reflect on the following verse of the Qur'an:

Alms are meant only for the poor, the needy, those who administer them, those whose hearts need winning over, to free slaves and help those in debt, for God's cause, and for travellers in need. This is ordained by God; God is all knowing and wise. (Al-Tawbah, 9:60)

Here are some essential questions we should be asking ourselves when giving:

- Do we donate most of our Zakat to the poor and needy in other countries that are less developed than our own, and where there is more suffering among our brothers and sisters? There are lots of strong and very good reasons to do this, with the most obvious reason being the concerningly limited access to rights, privileges and safety in comparison to our own.

- Do we make a note of the causes that mean something to us and we would like to support? How often do we review or revise these choices, depending on the progress of these charitable projects and our new goals?

- Have you considered the brothers and sisters that are suffering closer to home when giving charity? There are many people in our own country who are also suffering and struggling without our knowing, so it's worth doing your research, speaking to your local mosque and members of your community, and finding out if there's a need or way for you to help those less fortunate in your community.

- Is there anyone in our immediate family that classifies for Zakat?

- Reflecting on the verse above, have we thought of those 'whose hearts need winning over'? For example, reverts who may have been abandoned by their family will likely need us to help and support them in settling into a new community, until they can sufficiently look after themselves.

- When people reach out to us, do we just dismiss them, or do we extend our empathy and consider the likelihood that they may be asking us because they are in genuine need of our help?

- There are some Muslims who do not feel entirely comfortable giving money to charitable organisations that distribute aid due to the stigma that they may use a high percentage on their own administration costs. However, we do need to consider 'those who administer' help in our name. It is a great benefit to have organisations that distribute aid to those who need it and do all of the hard work on our behalf. Think of the those charity workers who tirelessly to raise charity for important causes during Ramadan, and those who travel to precarious locations to distribute emergency aid. We must remember that they need to be compensated for their efforts.

- Do we consider giving in God's cause? Have we ever considered contributing to the construction of a school or mosque where it is most needed? Or to facilities that help children and adults learn about Islam in an easy and accessible way, or help enhance people's Islamic knowledge ('ilm)?

These questions help us to focus on this essential pillar of the faith and have a more thoughtful approach to it. Think of it this way: if you want to buy something important for yourself, your home or somebody else of importance, you are likely to spend some time browsing different products, do your research, check customer reviews, and weigh up the pros and cons. It's unlikely if the item is of importance, that you will purchase the first thing you set your eyes on. So why is giving charity to brothers and sisters within our Ummah any less different? Our Ummah is of importance, for we are one body. Help people attentively with your charity just as you would wanted to be assisted if you were the one in need. There are many charitable causes, food banks, and local initiatives run by local mosques, grocery stores, youth clubs, schools, and other members of your community that you could get involved with.

The wealth you gain in the afterlife will be determined by how you used your own in this world. So use it wisely. Keep your heart open and empathetic, and engage with the plight of the Ummah.

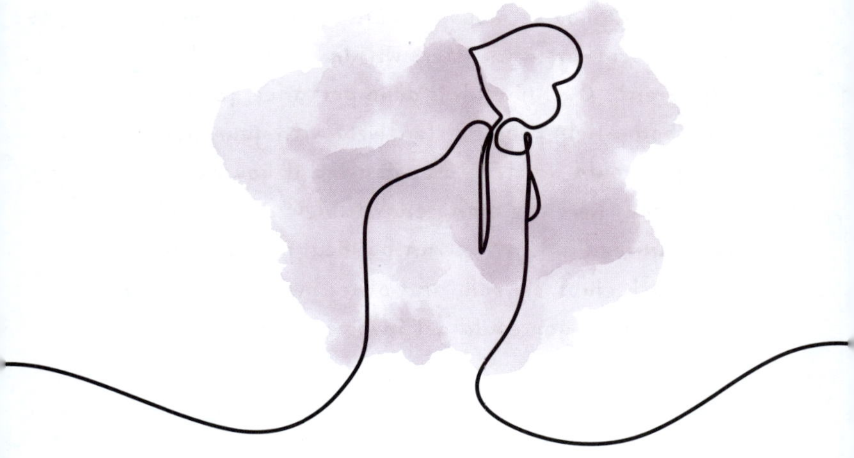

Life has a way of coming full circle. The love and care you put out into the world will return to you in ways better than you can imagine.

Charity comes in all shapes and sizes

Giving charity is not just donating money

There are numerous other ways to be charitable, such as being kind; being considerate and supportive of one another; using words of encouragement; smiling at others in a warm manner; sharing beneficial knowledge; showing kindness to our neighbours regardless of their faith or creed; offering your undivided attention to somebody who needs it, however young or old; being a good shoulder to cry on, or a good listener to someone who needs someone to talk to; being gentle and generous with your parents, spouse, and children; being caring towards animals. The list is endless.

All you need to do is get a little creative and resourceful. Develop the charity mindset from a young age if you have children of your own or younger siblings, and model what beautiful charity looks like, so that our children can mirror the generosity and empathy they see you give others in their own character.

Everyone has some capacity to give charity, regardless of their wealth.

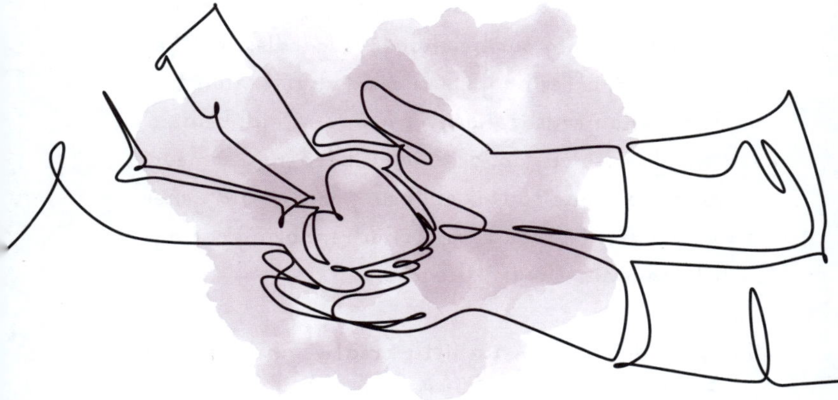

Being sympathetic and giving is an essential part of our humanity.

- I pray that Allah ﷿ makes us people of the Qur'an, heals us with His light and instils a deep love for our religion in our hearts—a love that makes us want to pick up His book and experience solace in its recitation and reflection. I pray that Allah ﷿ allows us to act upon its messages and for it to be a source of immense peace and guidance for us. I pray that we are driven and dedicated to making the very most out of Ramadan, whether we are able to fast or not, and that we are given the wisdom and discipline to take care of our overall health and mental well-being to enable a more positive experience of worship.

- I pray that Allah ﷿ grants us the motivation to pray salah and worship Him with full concentration, five times a day. I pray that He gives us the strength and determination to search for the night of Laylat al-Qadr, and that He allows us to maximise the opportunity of this night. I pray that we witness the beauty of Laylat al-Qadr, and that it becomes a source of immense blessing for us in the present and future. I pray that we are engaged with those who are less fortunate around us, that we give charity more mindfully, and make an effort to be charitable in more ways than one in Ramadan and beyond.

Ameen

Du'as for Ramadan

Abu Huraira ﷺ narrated Allah's Messenger ﷺ said: *"There are three whose supplication is not rejected: The fasting person when he breaks his fast, the just leader, and the supplication of the oppressed person; Allah raises it up above the clouds and opens the gates of heaven to it. And the Lord says: 'By My might, I shall surely aid you, even if it should be after a while.'"* (Tirmidhi)

If you are opening your fast with family or friends, take a few minutes to supplicate together, being grateful for Allah's ﷻ numerous mercies, the fast, and each other's presence. It's a nice habit to introduce, especially with children. If, for some reason, you didn't get to make your supplications, don't despair—it's never too late in the day to do them.

Firstly, let's start off with the supplications at the time of opening your fast:

ذَهَبَ الظَّمَأُ وَابْتَلَّتِ الْعُرُوقُ وَثَبَتَ الأَجْرُ
إِنْ شَاءَ اللهُ

Dhahabaẓ-ẓama', wabtallatil 'urūq, wa thabatal ajru inshā'Allāh

Thirst is gone, the veins are moistened and the reward is certain if Allah wills. (Abu Dawud)

اللَّهُمَّ اِنِّيْ لَكَ صُمْتُ وَبِكَ اٰمنْتُ وَعَلَى
رِزْقِكَ اَفْطَرْتُ

Allahumma innī laka ṣumtu, wa bika āmantu, wa 'ala rizqika afṭartu

Oh Allah! I fasted for You and I believe in You and I break my fast with Your sustenance.
(Abu Dawud)

Supplications you can pray in addition to these essential opening words are as follows. Remember to ask sincerely, with meaning and from the depths of our hearts:

رَبَّنَآ ءَاتِنَا فِى ٱلدُّنْيَا حَسَنَةً وَفِى ٱلْـَٔاخِرَةِ حَسَنَةً وَقِنَا عَذَابَ ٱلنَّارِ

Rabbanā ātina fid dunya ḥasanatan wa fil ākhirati ḥasanatan wa qinā ʿadhabān nār

Our Lord, give us good in this world and in the Hereafter, and protect us from the torment of the Fire. (Al-Baqarah, 2:201)

رَبَّنَا تَقَبَّلْ مِنَّآ ۖ إِنَّكَ أَنتَ ٱلسَّمِيعُ ٱلْعَلِيمُ

Rabbanā taqabbal minnā innaka antas samī ʿul ʿalīm

Our Lord, accept [this] from us, You are the All Hearing, the All Knowing. (Al-Baqarah, 2:127)

رَبَّنَا لَا تُؤَاخِذْنَآ إِن نَّسِينَآ أَوْ أَخْطَأْنَا ۚ رَبَّنَا
وَلَا تَحْمِلْ عَلَيْنَآ إِصْرًا كَمَا حَمَلْتَهُۥ عَلَى
ٱلَّذِينَ مِن قَبْلِنَا ۚ رَبَّنَا وَلَا تُحَمِّلْنَا مَا لَا طَاقَةَ
لَنَا بِهِۦ ۖ وَٱعْفُ عَنَّا وَٱغْفِرْ لَنَا وَٱرْحَمْنَآ ۚ أَنتَ
مَوْلَىٰنَا فَٱنصُرْنَا عَلَى ٱلْقَوْمِ ٱلْكَٰفِرِينَ

Rabbanā lā tu'ākhidhnā in nasīnā aw akhtānā; rabbanā wa lā taḥmil-'alaynā iṣran kamā ḥamaltahū 'alal-ladhīna min qablinā; rabbanā wa lā tuḥammilnā mā lā ṭāqata lanā bih; wa'fu 'annā waghfir lanā warḥamnā; anta mawlānā fanṣurnā 'alal qawmil kāfirīn

Our Lord! Do not punish us if we forget or make a mistake. Our Lord! Do not place a burden on us like the one you placed on those before us. Our Lord! Do not burden us with what we cannot bear. Pardon us, forgive us, and have mercy on us. You are our only Guardian. So grant us victory over the disbelieving people.

(Al-Baqarah, 2:286)

رَبَّنَا لَا تُزِغْ قُلُوبَنَا بَعْدَ إِذْ هَدَيْتَنَا وَهَبْ لَنَا مِن لَّدُنكَ رَحْمَةً ۚ إِنَّكَ أَنتَ ٱلْوَهَّابُ

Rabbanā lā tuzigh qulūbanā ba'da idh hadaytanā wa hab lanā mil ladunka raḥmah; innaka antal wahhāb

Our Lord, do not let our hearts deviate after You have guided us. Grant us your mercy: You are the Ever Giving. (Al-'Imran, 3:8)

رَبَّنَآ إِنَّنَآ ءَامَنَّا فَٱغْفِرْ لَنَا ذُنُوبَنَا وَقِنَا عَذَابَ ٱلنَّارِ

Rabbanā innanā āmannā faghfir lanā dhunūbanā wa qinā 'adhāban nār

Our Lord, we believe so forgive us our sins and protect us from suffering in the Fire.
(Al-'Imran, 3:16)

رَبَّنَا فَٱغْفِرْ لَنَا ذُنُوبَنَا وَكَفِّرْ عَنَّا سَيِّـَٔاتِنَا وَتَوَفَّنَا مَعَ ٱلْأَبْرَارِ

Rabbanā faghfir lanā dhunūbanā wa kaffir ʻannā sayyiātinā wa tawaffanā maʻal abrār

Our Lord! Forgive us our sins, wipe out our bad deeds, and grant that we join the righteous when we die. (Al-'Imran, 3:193)

رَبَّنَا ظَلَمْنَآ أَنفُسَنَا وَإِن لَّمْ تَغْفِرْ لَنَا وَتَرْحَمْنَا لَنَكُونَنَّ مِنَ ٱلْخَٰسِرِينَ

Rabbanā ẓalamnā anfusanā wa illam taghfir lanā wa tarḥamnā lanakūnanna minal khāsirīn

Our Lord, we have wronged our souls: if You do not forgive us and have mercy, we shall be lost. (Al-A'raf, 7:23)

وَقُلْ رَّبِّ اغْفِرْ وَارْحَمْ وَاَنْتَ خَيْرُ الرّٰحِمِيْنَ

Rabbigh fir warḥam wa anta khayrur rāhimīn

My Lord, forgive me and have mercy, and you are the best, most merciful. (Al-Mu'minun, 23:118)

رَبَّنَا وَسِعْتَ كُلَّ شَىْءٍ رَّحْمَةً وَعِلْمًا فَٱغْفِرْ
لِلَّذِينَ تَابُوا۟ وَٱتَّبَعُوا۟ سَبِيلَكَ وَقِهِمْ عَذَابَ
ٱلْجَحِيمِ. رَبَّنَا وَأَدْخِلْهُمْ جَنَّٰتِ عَدْنٍ ٱلَّتِى
وَعَدتَّهُمْ وَمَن صَلَحَ مِنْ ءَابَآئِهِمْ وَأَزْوَٰجِهِمْ
وَذُرِّيَّٰتِهِمْ ۚ إِنَّكَ أَنتَ ٱلْعَزِيزُ ٱلْحَكِيمُ

Rabbanā wasi'ta kulla shay'ir raḥmataw wa 'ilman faghfir lilladhīna tabū wattaba'ū sabīlaka wa qihim 'adhābal-jaḥīm Rabbanā wa adkhilhum jannāti 'adnin allati wa 'attahum wa man ṣalaḥa min ābā'ihim wa azwājihim wa dhurriyyātihim, innaka antal 'azizul-ḥakim

Lord, you embrace all things in mercy and knowledge, so forgive those who turn to You and follow Your path. Save them from the pains of Hell and admit them, Lord, to the lasting Gardens You have promised to them, together with the righteous ancestors, spouses, and offspring. You alone have the power to decide.

(Al-Mu'min, 40:7-8)

Here are some beautiful supplications of our beloved Prophet ﷺ, the best of mankind. These are good examples for us to follow in addition to our own, heartfelt supplications:

لَا إِلَهَ إِلَّا اللَّهُ وَحْدَهُ لَا شَرِيكَ لَهُ لَهُ الْمُلْكُ
وَلَهُ الْحَمْدُ وَهُوَ عَلَى كُلِّ شَيْءٍ قَدِيرٌ

Lā ilāha illallāh, waḥdahū lā sharīka lahū, lahul mulku wa lahul-ḥamdu, wa huwa ʻalā kulli shay'in qadīr

None has the right to be worshipped but Allah, the Alone Who has no partners, to Him belongs Dominion and to Him belong all the Praises, and He has power over all things. (Bukhari)

Shadaad ibn 'Aws رضي الله عنه narrated that the Prophet ﷺ said: *"The best supplication for seeking forgiveness (Syed al-Istighfar) is to say:*

اللّٰهُمَّ أَنْتَ رَبِّي، لَا إِلٰهَ إِلَّا أَنْتَ، خَلَقْتَنِيْ
وَأَنَا عَبْدُكَ، وَأَنَا عَلَى عَهْدِكَ وَوَعْدِكَ مَا
اسْتَطَعْتُ، أَعُوْذُ بِكَ مِنْ شَرِّ مَا صَنَعْتُ،
أَبُوءُ لَكَ بِنِعْمَتِكَ عَلَيَّ وَأَبُوءُ بِذَنْبِيْ، فَاغْفِرْ
لِيْ، فَإِنَّهُ لَا يَغْفِرُ الذُّنُوْبَ إِلَّا أَنْتَ

Allahumma anta rabbī, lā ilāha illā anta, khalaqtanī wa anā 'abduka, wa anā 'ala 'ahdika wa wa'dika mastaṭa'tu, a'ūdhu bika min sharri ma ṣana'tu, abū'u laka bini'matika 'alayya, wa abū'u bidhanbī faghfir lī, fa innahū lā yaghfirudh-dhunūba illā anta

O Allah! You are my Lord. There is no true god except You. You have created me, and I am Your slave, and I hold to Your Covenant as far as I can. I seek refuge in You from the evil of what I have done. I acknowledge the favours that You have bestowed upon me, and I confess my sins. Pardon me, for none but You has the power to pardon.

He who supplicates in these terms during the day with firm belief in it and dies on the same day (before the evening), he will be one of the dwellers of Jannah; and if anyone supplicates in these terms during the night with firm belief in it and dies before the morning, he will be one of the dwellers of Jannah." (Riyad as-Salihin)

We can send salutations on the Prophet ﷺ as we have been commanded in the Qur'an:

اللّٰهُمَّ صَلِّ عَلٰى مُحَمَّدٍ وَّعَلٰٓى اٰلِ مُحَمَّدٍ كَمَا
صَلَّيْتَ عَلٰٓى إِبْرَاهِيمَ وَعَلٰى اٰلِ إِبْرَاهِيمَ
اِنَّكَ حَمِيْدٌ مَّجِيْدٌ اللّٰهُمَّ بَارِكْ عَلٰى مُحَمَّدٍ
وَّعَلٰٓى اٰلِ مُحَمَّدٍ كَمَا بَارَكْتَ عَلٰٓى إِبْرَاهِيمَ
وَعَلٰٓى اٰلِ إِبْرَاهِيمَ اِنَّكَ حَمِيْدٌ مَّجِيْدٌ

Allahumma ṣalli ʿala Muḥammadin wa ʿala āli Muḥammadin kamā ṣallayta ʿala Ibrāhīma wa ʿala āli Ibrāhīma innaka ḥamīdum majīd. Allahumma bārik ʿala Muḥammadin wa ʿala āli Muḥammadin kamā bārakta ʿala Ibrāhīma wa ʿala āli Ibrāhīma innaka ḥamīdum majīd

O Allah, let Your Blessings come upon Muhammad ﷺ and the family of Muhammad ﷺ, as you have blessed Ibrahim and his family. Truly, You are Praiseworthy and Glorious. Allah, bless Muhammad and the family of Muhammad, as you have blessed Ibrahim and his family. Truly, You are Praiseworthy and Glorious. (Muslim)

Farewell, dear Ramadan?

We've been on a spiritual high this month, and have felt some really positive, spiritual growth from within. But it's time for Ramadan to leave us, much like a beloved family member whom we have cherished the company of.

How are you feeling now that the end is nearing?

Sad? Nervous? Exhausted? Excited to embrace the new you?

It's getting close to Eid, and we are often asked by our non-fasting friends and colleagues if we are excited that Ramadan is nearly over, so that we can finally eat and drink. But...

- How do we express that although we look forward to Eid, we feel a deep sadness that Ramadan has passed so quickly?

- How do we explain that despite our efforts, we may still feel that we could have strived for more?

- How do we explain that when we are debating when Eid is, we take a sigh of relief when we realise that Allah ﷻ has blessed us with another day to fast when the moon has not been sighted?

- How do we express that as Ramadan is nearing its end, we have tears in our eyes and our hearts are filled with the inner peace, light and barakah of this month, and that we are already longing for the next one?

- How do we explain that we are feeling slightly nervous about the idea of recalibrating 'back to normal life', when we know deep in our soul that we are now in a **new** phase of spiritual development, and want to keep moving **forwards** rather than backwards?

While you may be feeling some very mixed emotions right now, remind yourself that the feeling of sadness or nervousness is a positive sign.

- It is a sign that Ramadan has touched your heart and nourished your soul.
- It is a sign that you have made some positive changes to your worship this month.
- It is a sign that you have become closer to Allah ﷻ.
- It is a sign that you want to continue growing as a Muslim, and setting yourself a new goal for living after Ramadan.

Harness the mixed emotions that you are feeling into motivation, making it your new goal to be proactive in your spiritual development well beyond Ramadan.

Shawwal—
A time for renewal

It's the first day of Shawwal—'Eid Mubarak!

'Eid signifies the continuation of all of the good deeds we have done in the blessed month of Ramadan. Shawwal is a month of new beginnings, and a further strengthening of the new self we have developed over the last month. And yet, as we gather with our loved ones on the exciting day of 'Eid, the celebrations of the day distract us and make us lose sight of the first day of the blessed month of Shawwal.

We may have experienced or at least seen things like this at some point in time, despite our good intentions:

- Being completely exhausted after the final fast and sleeping through Fajr prayer on 'Eid morning.
- Cooking too much food so that there's plenty left over, some of which may go to waste.
- Not being mindful about how much we are eating.
- Watching too much TV, listening to music or catching up with social media because you've missed engaging with them for the last thirty days. Often it is only after a break from these that our newly-calibrated, spiritual selves realise how inappropriate some of the content can be.
- Not getting around to reading any Qur'an on the day of 'Eid.
- If you are a Muslimah, you may excitedly put on nail varnish and make up, and not want to remove this when it is salah time and you have to do your wudu, so you miss your prayers or intentionally delay them.

- You spend a lot of time getting ready for 'Eid or spending time in your room, not being considerate of the workload of those who are hosting 'Eid and preparing all the food on their own.

Does the list go on?

To be fair, we feel we deserve a break after being so devoted for a month and we want to enjoy the celebration of 'Eid. And we should!

Allah ﷻ grants us the relief of 'Eid as a day of celebrating our Ramadan journey with loved ones who have shared it with us. However, what small things could we do on the day of 'Eid to keep the spirit of Ramadan alive, rather than quickly forgetting the beautiful forms of worship that we made a conscious effort to implement during the last thirty days?

Here are a few suggestions:

- Remember to have paid your Zakat al-Fitr before 'Eid prayers, so that everyone around us has the opportunity to celebrate 'Eid by having a meal to eat.

- Make a conscious effort to start your day positively by getting up to read Fajr. It's day one of Shawwal, a time for renewal—not a day of forgetfulness. You're naturally very distracted today and recovering from long nights of worship; but think of it like this: you still get an extra bit of sleep as you don't have to get up earlier for the pre-morning meal, and you do not want to undo your hard work over Ramadan as soon as the month has finished, for the goal to pray salah should be permanent. If you feel that you may struggle with this, use some of the tips covered in the Ramadan section to help you successfully wake up for Fajr salah, or read your salah on time.

- For those that are able to attend 'Eid prayer in congregation in the morning, as you get ready to go to the mosque, try and make an effort in how you present yourself for prayer. If you have the means to, wear fresh, new clothes, or at least wear the best clothes that you have; apply 'attar (men only); perform ghusl (ritual purification); and groom yourself in order celebrate your growth this Ramadan, and to honour the new person you have become as a result of it. These were the sunnahs of the Prophet ﷺ on 'Eid. This also honours the day of 'Eid and shows our gratitude to Allah ﷻ for His blessings.

Children of Adam, dress well whenever you are at worship, and eat and drink (as We have permitted) but do not be extravagant: God does not like extravagant people. (Al-A'raf, 7:31)

- It is prohibited to fast on the day of 'Eid. Anas ibn Malik ؓ narrated that Allah's Messenger ﷺ would eat an odd number of dates before leaving for 'Eid prayer (Bukhari).

- The Prophet ﷺ would walk and go out on the day of 'Eid by one route, and he would return by another (Bukhari). This might not sound important, but we should try to follow it if we can. There are so many good reasons why the Prophet ﷺ did this and one of them is that by changing our path, we are open to Allah ﷻ changing our condition and that is really what our spiritual journey has been about (Bukhari).

- Why not pray your other salah in congregation together, to help you all still feel connected to the shared experience of worship?

- Can you make an effort to implement something that you did in Ramadan again on 'Eid, to keep up the continuity of your practices? For example, if you did a prayer before opening your fast, could you share a prayer before feasting on all the 'Eid delights? If you used to spend five minutes on the prayer mat after your salah doing dhikr, could you make sure you do the same again today? If you started to begin and end your day with a certain du'a or positive habit, could you repeat this on 'Eid day? If you are pressed for time, could you replace the actions at those times with something that is less time-consuming today, but is still meaningful, to keep the feeling of the habit consistent in your mind?

- 'Eid is celebrated with families and friends spending time together and making more happy memories. Meet with as many people as you can and make the effort to reach out to those who live further away from you through phone or video calls, to show your love and respect to them on this special day.

- Follow the essence of Ramadan by cooking quantities that can all be eaten, to prevent wastage. After fasting, we find our bodies do not allow us to consume as much as we might want to. This doesn't mean you can't prepare or have your favourite foods and delights; but it is important that we remember to be mindful and God-conscious when making decisions, whether you are hosting or attending as a guest.

- You could also send some food to your neighbours if you have the ability to do so, or invite a friend that may be celebrating alone.

Keep the spirit of Ramadan alive on 'Eid by remaining empathetic and considerate to those around you, as well as being diligent in maintaining that renewed God-consciousness.

Fasting in the month of Shawwal and beyond

Whilst fasting on the first day of Shawwal is prohibited due to the celebration of 'Eid, it is recommended to fast for six days during this month. Many choose to fast straight after 'Eid, while others find it easier to spread the days over the month.

Abu Ayyub al-Ansari ﷺ narrated that Allah's Messenger ﷺ said: *"Whoever fasts Ramadan then follows it with six days of Shawwal, it is as if he fasted for a lifetime."* (Muslim)

There are many other times of the year that you could perform voluntary fasting if this is something that you want to develop. For example:

- After the month of Shawwal, it is also recommended to **fast nine days prior to 'Eid al-Adha** in the month of **Dhul-Hijjah**. In particular on the ninth day, the day of 'Arafat, which is the day before 'Eid al-Adha.

- The month of Muharram, in particular on the **day of 'Ashura**, which falls on the tenth day of this month. This was the day our beloved Prophet Moses عليه السلام and the Children of Israel were saved from Pharaoh.

When the Prophet Muhammad ﷺ arrived at Madina, he noticed that some people among the Jews used to respect 'Ashura (10th Muharram) and fast on it. The Prophet ﷺ then said:

"We have more right to observe fast on this day."

and ordered that fasting should be observed on it (Bukhari).

Best days of the week:

Abu Huraira ﷺ narrated that Allah's Messenger ﷺ said: *"Deeds are presented on Monday and Thursday, and I love that my deeds be presented while I am fasting."* (Tirmidhi)

Best days of the month:

Qatada ibn Milhan ﷺ reported: *"The Messenger of Allah ﷺ directed us to observe fasting on the thirteenth, fourteenth and fifteenth of the (lunar) month."* (Abu Dawud).

These three days are known as the white days of the month when the moon is at its fullest.

I personally find that throughout the year we naturally have some dips. If I find myself in a situation where I start to struggle to get up for Fajr, and feel like it's becoming a pattern, I'll make the intention to fast. It might sound strange; however, I know that fasting is about being God-conscious, so I know that I'll get up before the start of Fajr and have something to eat before starting my fast. It helps to keep me on track.

If we want Allah ﷾ – Al-Fattah (The Opener) – to open the door of Ar-Raiyan for us, one of the gates of paradise, then fasting outside of Ramadan is a good practice.

The beautiful Names of Allah

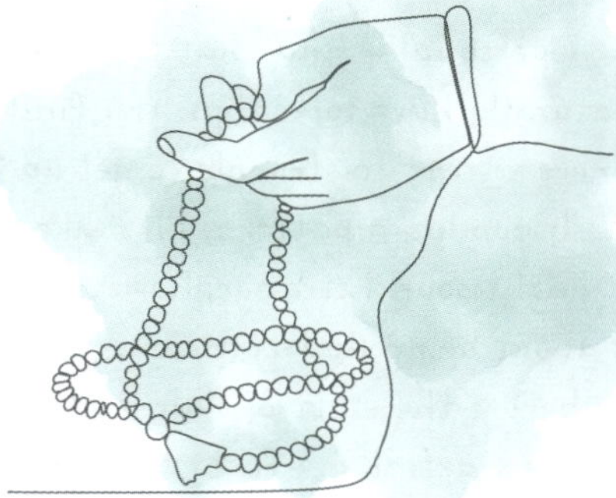

- During Sha'ban, we started off by supplicating with small yet powerful remembrances, like 'Subhan'Allah'.
- During Ramadan, we built on these with some longer supplications for forgiveness, and some inspiring, Prophetic supplications.
- During Shawwal and beyond, we can continue to develop our dhikr by also referring to Allah's ﷻ names in order to help us feel even closer to our Lord, and to strengthen our appreciation for His powerful and reassuring qualities.

[Prophet], if My servants ask you about Me, I am near. I respond to those who call Me, so let them respond to Me, and believe in Me, so that they may be guided. (Al-Baqarah, 2:186)

Get to know Allah ﷻ – supplicate using His Names

When we speak to our family members, our friends, or our colleagues, we usually learn about them as a person, and we take an interest in aspects of their personality. As we get to know someone, our relationship naturally develops with them as time goes on; the more we speak to each other, the closer we feel. One of the things that's helped me feel closer to Allah ﷻ is to learn about His Names and His Attributes.

Learn how to use His names in a meaningful way.

You can use His names when supplicating in general and during prostration in your prayers. Depending on your circumstance, select those of His names that are most appropriate to your situation, feeling and what you are seeking help for.

The Most Excellent Names belong to God; use them to call on Him, and keep away from those who abuse His names - they will be requited for what they do. (Al-A'raf, 7:180)

Here are some supplication examples you could use during your dhikr of Allah ﷻ:

الْوَدُودُ

Al-Wadūd

Ask the **'Most Loving'** to love and to be pleased with you. To fill your heart with love for Him, the Qur'an, the prophets and everything that He loves.

اَلْعَلِيْمُ

Al-'Alīm

Ask the **'All-Knowing'** to teach us what is beneficial to us and to benefit us from what we already know.

الْعَظِيمُ

Al-'Aẓīm

Ask **'The Magnificent One'** to give us the strength not to give up. To keep going and make the impossible, possible—beyond our imagination

الْقُدُّوسُ

Al-Quddūs

Ask the **'Absolutely Pure'** to cleanse our heart and soul from impurities.

الْفَتَّاحُ

Al-Fattāh

Ask 'The Opener' to open the doors to success for us, in this life and the next.

One of my personal favourite forms of praising Allah ﷻ is the following:

سُبْحَانَ اللهِ وَبِحَمْدِهِ عَدَدَ خَلْقِهِ، وَرِضا نَفْسِهِ، وَزِنَةَ عَرْشِهِ، وَمِدادَ كَلِماتِهِ

Subhān Allāhi wa biḥamdihī, 'adada khalqihī, wa riḍā nafsihī, wa zinatah 'arshihī, wa midada kalimātihī

Allah ﷻ is free from imperfection and I begin with His praise, as many times as the number of His creatures, in accordance with His Good Pleasure, equal to the weight of His Throne and equal to the ink that may be used in recording the words (for His Praise). (Muslim)

For those of you that may want to develop your supplications as a new goal for your spiritual development, you could start to look at the morning and evening forms of remembrance and praise.

Naturally, when we need help, we supplicate to Allah ﷻ, as we should, since help comes from Him alone. Though in times of ease, it is easy to become somewhat complacent in our state of contentment. This is the time where we should be mindful of extending our supplication in praise and gratitude for Allah's ﷻ blessings upon us.

Keep up your supplications after Ramadan, little by little, for we must keep the tongue moist and the mind focused with daily remembrance of The One who loves us most.

The post-Ramadan mindset

Shawwal can be considered a month of 'renewal' because we come out of Ramadan feeling more spiritually connected. Shawwal can be the month that helps us move forward with more drive and determination, with new goals in mind, as we have now unlocked our potential, and have tasted what a deeper spiritual connection can feel like.

Like the new buds of a plant that reveal themselves in Spring, you are now able to witness and feel the fresh buds of a deeper connection with Allah ﷻ again.

There may be elements of your spiritual practice that you feel proud of because you have started to implement them mindfully, or are now more consistent with certain acts of worship than you used to be. That is amazing, masha'Allah.

But there are also things you know in your heart you could still work on, or perhaps didn't pay enough attention to.

Don't lose hope.

You still have time to plant those seeds and nurture that part of your growth after Ramadan.

So what are you waiting for?

Ramadan might have ended, but this is your new beginning.

Make the intention for continued growth in Shawwal, and set some new goals.

And watch how you grow, and grow, and grow.

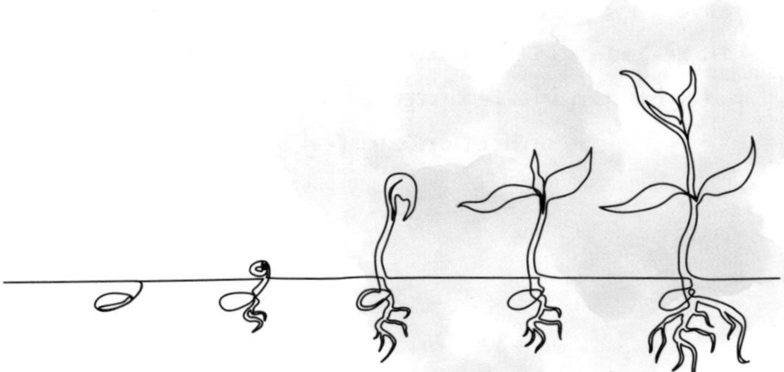

Indeed,
Allah will not change the condition of a people until they change what is in themselves.

(Al-R'ad, 13:11)

Reflecting on your growth

So how are we going to integrate back into our busy lives with a much stronger feeling of purpose?
How are we going to keep that spiritual connection **alive?**
How do we move forward after such a purifying and soul-searching month?

Our journey together from Sha'ban to Ramadan in this book has prompted us time and time again to be more present and mindful in our actions, to make clear and sincere intentions, and to set reasonable and practical goals for spiritual development.

Before you start thinking about your next steps, spend a little time reviewing and reflecting on your wholesome journey from the month of Sha'ban to now:

What do you feel is different about you?

What growth have you seen in yourself?

How does this change make you feel?

What types of spiritual practice(s) do you hope continues well after Ramadan?

If there were a couple of things you could say to the version of yourself that existed before Sha'ban, what would you say?

You could do this reflection exercise on your own, together as a family, and/or within your social circles to motivate each other and stay accountable.

If you can see that others are struggling to maintain consistency beyond Ramadan, do not judge them. You often hear the term 'Ramadan Muslims'—those that devote themselves only during the month, but then struggle to practise diligently afterwards.

Allah سبحانه وتعالى gave us all the ability to worship and do good in the blessed month, and this month proves that we all really do have the ability within us to devote ourselves. We just have to make the effort to learn and unlock that potential that we have.

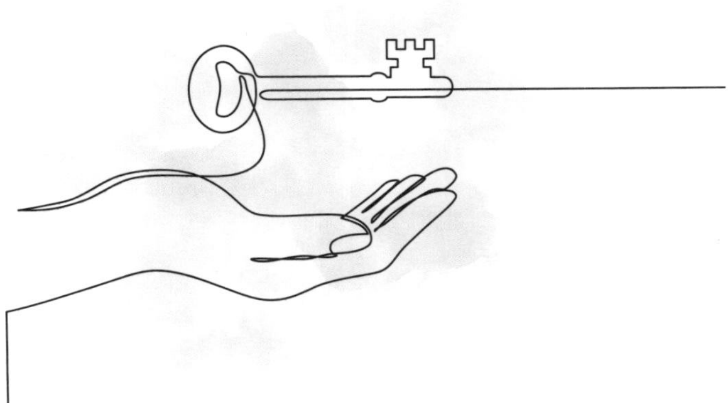

Let's help and encourage each other to continue as best we can beyond Ramadan. All change is positive no matter how small you may think it is. We all have highs and lows, but keep on trying! That intention and that effort for positive change is the key. Don't give up hope, and know that everything is in Allah's ﷾ Hands. As humans, we are often quick to focus on the negatives—ours and other people's—but let's celebrate and focus on what positive changes we have made this year, and pick each other up!

Your spiritual growth

The garment of God-consciousness is the best of all garments this is one of God's signs, so that people may take heed. (Surah Al-A'raf, 7:26)

Use the checklist below to track your spiritual progress, and to help you visualise your efforts over time. This can be used during the three blessed months and throughout the year, and can be revised several times, as the growth of a Muslim never stops.

Lessons for me to try and put into practice for my eternal blossoming...

I am transforming my 'Ramadan Mindset', so that I work on preparing for my renewal **before** Ramadan

I will avoid eating with greed, or indulging in frequently unhealthy ingredients leading up to and during Ramadan

I am making more positive use of my time and talk in social gatherings

I am being more selective with what I see, listen to and share on my device

I am making an effort to settle disputes and ask for forgiveness

I am making an effort to wake up for suhoor during Ramadan

I am more mindful of the quality of my spiritual engagement, rather than just the quantity of my actions

I am more mindful of how I purify my body for prayer through wudu

I am making a conscious and dedicated effort to pray my salah as a matter of priority

I am preparing carefully for Fajr prayer to help me wake up

I am being more mindful of how I use my hands to support others around me both inside and outside of the home, and when connecting with Allah ﷻ in prayer

I need to make a sincere intention for this and actually start the process	I have just started practising this. I pray I remain consistent. Ameen!	I am actually making good progress with this, alhamdulillah!

Lessons for me to try and put into practice for my eternal blossoming...

I am being more considerate, selective and mindful of my words, both in spoken and written form

I am engaging in more du'a and dhikr of Allah ﷻ throughout my day

I am making a more conscious effort to increase/ diversify my acts of charity, however big or small

I am remembering to be kind to myself, and prioritise the values of Ramadan, if I decide to host or feed others

(Brothers) I am making a conscious effort to attend the masjid to attend congregational prayer

(Sisters) I am attempting to connect with Allah ﷻ in alternative ways when menstruating/ not fasting

I am transforming my 'Ramadan Mindset', so that I work on growing beyond Ramadan

I am God-conscious on 'Eid day, despite the celebratory distractions, by making an effort to worship Allah ﷻ diligently

I make an effort to fast during Shawwal

I am trying my best to instil the spiritual practices I embedded in Sha'ban, Ramadan and Shawwal throughout the year

I need to make a sincere intention for this and actually start the process	I have just started practising this. I pray I remain consistent. Ameen!	I am actually making good progress with this, alhamdulillah!

Remember that each day, each week and each month is a stepping stone. Take one goal at a time, and master that goal for at least thirty to forty days before moving on the next one. Depending on what your goal is, you might need more time for that practice to truly flourish. And that's okay.

As we've said before, don't worry about quantity. Focus on the **quality** of your worship. Devise a plan on how you are going to reasonably and practically implement this practice more consistently in your life, and review your progress in these areas throughout the year. Over the weeks, months and years, you will look back and see how much you have blossomed, insha'Allah.

Put the effort in now, and have full trust in the fact that Allah ﷾ is Most Merciful. The results only ever come from Him alone, through His Mercy and Plan for you.

Another thing I found very useful was surrounding myself with like-minded people who had similar motivations and goals. If you share this self-review with others, you actively participate in each other's spiritual growth and gently guide each other to success, checking in with each other on specific practices, such as reading salah on time. These people could be your family members or your friends, or it could be people you meet through Islamic classes or circles. But you don't have to share your progress with anyone else, if you don't want to. It can just be between you and Allah ﷻ.

Goals for the future

Ramadan is a glimpse
of what you are truly able to achieve

The growth never stops

The sign of an accepted Ramadan and Shawwal is one where the months have touched our heart in some way, motivating us to continue to do good afterwards. All you need is the right mindset, a clear plan, and some perseverance. It might sometimes feel hard to achieve that level of connection you felt in Ramadan and Shawwal again with so many worldly distractions in the way, but trying is the first step to achieving positive change. It's only natural that we feel we won't be able to sustain the same level of dedication as we did in Ramadan; however, it is not impossible. Can we make some positive steps towards more growth or re-growth, rather than abandoning our goals altogether?

It's not a race. Take one step at a time. It's not reasonable to unlearn the behaviours and habits that have developed over years, overnight. Development and growth take time and commitment. The growth never stops. It doesn't matter how much you think you have achieved. A true and humble believer knows that they can always do more.

Considering all of the things that we have covered in this book and on the spiritual growth you have seen so far after Shawwal, set for yourself three clear and realistic goals for yourself for the rest of the year.

How will you strive to be a better version of yourself between now and the next Ramadan? What will you do (differently)?

1

2

3

A final prayer for the Ummah

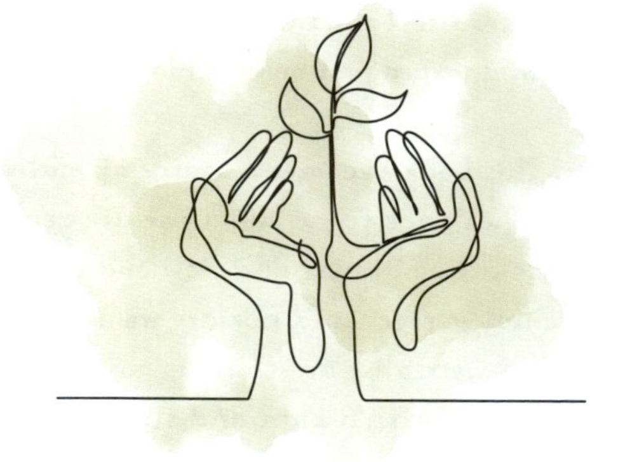

- As we embark on a future, feeling renewed, I pray to Allah ﷻ that the seeds we planted in Sha'ban , grew in Ramadan and developed in Shawwal will bloom throughout the entire year. I pray that we reflect in these months and move forward by setting goals for the rest of the year—goals that continue to bring us closer to Allah ﷻ and everything that He loves.

- I pray that we are able to perform good deeds on a consistent basis, and that we continue to connect with revelation, worship Him with sincerity and from the depths of our hearts. I pray that we continue to seek knowledge and act upon the lessons we learn, and that we strive to be like the best of mankind, our beloved Prophet ﷺ – a Prophet that sacrificed everything for us and prayed for his entire Ummah. I pray that we meet him in Paradise, have the honour of opening our fasts with him and praying behind him.

✿ I pray that this book becomes a source of motivation, comfort and guidance for us all, as we are gently reminded of our humanness and how change takes time; we are not perfect and nor are we expected to be. I pray that we realise anything is possible if we align our thoughts with a plan and start our plan with sincere intention and du'a for productivity. I pray that we choose not to give up when things are not working the way we want them to, and that we keep trying to commit to acts of worship for the sake of our connection with Allah ﷻ. I pray that we turn to Him first and foremost, rely on Him and know that everything including success is from Him alone. I pray that Allah ﷻ gives us the ability to strive in His path, to help and guide others. I pray that He makes us amongst those servants that are most beloved to Him and raises us to a highly praised status.

- Finally, I pray that, over time, we can all flower into beautiful, persevering, strong and generous Muslims who can enjoy the scented gardens of Jannah as a lasting reward for our consistent efforts in this world, despite our imperfections.

Ameen

"Every time a person finishes an act of worship, he should seek Allah's forgiveness for his shortcomings, and thank Him for enabling him to do it. He should not be like one who thinks that he has perfected his acts of worship and done a favour to his Lord..." (Tafsir as-Sa'di)

I pray that this book
becomes a source of
blessing for us both

Nabeelah

Kristallhöhlen
Zerklüftete Ber
Blubbernder Sumpf
Schlafsee
Das Schattenland
Blaue Bucht
Feuerinsel

Katrina Charman

Der letzte Feuerfalke und der geheimnisvolle See

Band 4

Bisher erschienen:

Band 1: Der letzte Feuerfalke und der Stein der Macht
Band 2: Der letzte Feuerfalke und die Kristallhöhlen
Band 3: Der letzte Feuerfalke und die flüsternde Eiche
Band 4: Der letzte Feuerfalke und der geheimnisvolle See

Katrina Charman

DER LETZTE FEUERFALKE

und der geheimnisvolle See

Band 4

Illustriert von Jeremy Norton

Aus dem Amerikanischen übersetzt von
Klaus Mende und Sabine Tandetzke

Loewe

Für Maddie, Piper und Riley. – KC
Ich danke meinen Eltern, die mir gezeigt haben, wie wertvoll Kunst ist. – JN

FSC
www.fsc.org
MIX
Papier aus verantwortungsvollen Quellen
FSC® C014496

ISBN 978-3-7432-0815-5
1. Auflage 2022
erschienen unter dem Originaltitel
The last firehawk – Lullaby Lake

Published by Arrangement with SCHOLASTIC INC.,
557 Broadway, New York, NY 10012 USA
Dieses Werk wurde vermittelt durch die Literarische Agentur
Thomas Schlück GmbH, 30161 Hannover.
Für die deutschsprachige Ausgabe

Aus dem Amerikanischen übersetzt von Sabine Tandetzke und Klaus Mende
Umschlag- und Innenillustrationen: Jeremy Norton
Umschlaggestaltung: Ramona Karl
Printed in the EU

www.loewe-verlag.de

Inhalt

Prolog

Im verborgenen Land Perodia liegt der Wald von Valor – ein Ort voller Magie und Licht. Dort führt eine weise alte Eule namens Grey die Eulen von Valor an. Diese tapferen Kämpfer beschützen die Geschöpfe des Waldes. Doch eine unheimliche Dunkelheit breitet sich über Perodia aus und lässt die Magie des Waldes und das Licht verblassen …

Der mächtige alte Geier Burung herrscht über den *Schatten*, einen dunklen Zauber. Immer wenn der *Schatten* erscheint, sind Burung und seine Armee rotäugiger Spione nicht fern. Und er wird nicht aufhören, ehe Perodia zerstört ist. Nur

mit dem magischen Stein der Macht könnte es gelingen, Burung ein für alle Mal aufzuhalten. Talon, eine kleine Schleiereule, und seine Freunde Agila, ein flinkes Eichhörnchen, und Ruby, der letzte Feuerfalke, machen sich auf die Suche. Sie haben bereits drei der Stücke vom Stein der Macht gefunden, die an verschiedenen Orten in Perodia versteckt sind. Aber immer noch fehlen Teile. Burung und seine Spione suchen ebenfalls nach dem Stein der Macht – und nach Ruby. Die aufregende Reise der Freunde geht weiter …

Auf zum Schlafsee!

Talon und seine Freunde Agila und Ruby standen am Fuß der Mooshügel. Die Landschaft um sie herum war vertrocknet. Die Bäume und Büsche, die Burung und der *Schatten* zerstört hatten, waren braun.

„Wir müssen zum Schlafsee, um das nächste Stück vom Stein der Macht zu finden", sagte Talon. Er betrachtete den hellen Punkt auf der magischen Landkarte, die Grey ihnen gegeben hatte.

Agila zeigte auf ein dunkelbraunes Gebiet auf der Karte. Es lag zwischen den Mooshügeln und dem See. „Was ist das?“, fragte sie.

Talon las den Namen von der Karte ab. „Der Blubbernde Sumpf.“ Ruby beugte sich über seine Schulter. Er konnte kaum glauben, wie groß seine Freundin geworden war. Inzwischen überragte sie ihn und Agila und hatte viele neue Wörter gelernt. Außerdem besaß sie erstaunliche Kräfte: die Macht über das Feuer, superstarke Flügel und einen lauten Schrei, der alle Feinde vertrieb. Talon lächelte. Er war froh, einen Feuerfalken an seiner Seite zu haben.

Ruby tippte mit ihrem Schnabel auf die Landkarte. „Burung!“, rief sie.

„Ruby hat recht“, sagte Agila. „Der See liegt dicht beim Schattenland. Und dort haust Burung.“

„Wir werden uns so weit nördlich wie möglich halten“, erwiderte Talon.

Er schaute in die Höhe und hielt nach dem *Schatten* Ausschau, aber der Himmel war klar.

Bis jetzt.

„Wir sollten uns auf den Weg machen“, sagte er. „Burung und seine Spione kommen näher. In der Luft sind wir schneller, also sollten wir lieber fliegen.“

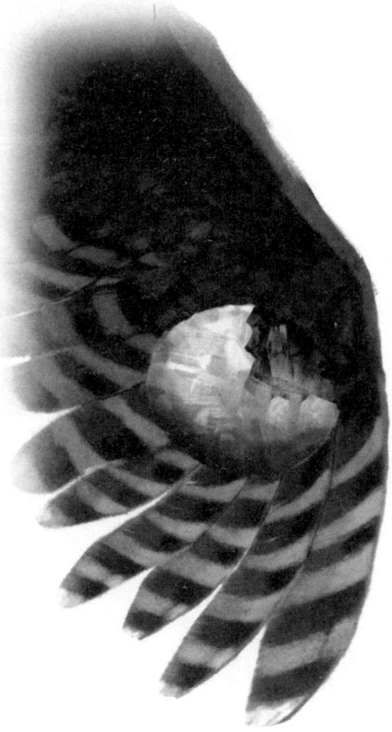

Agila nickte und kletterte auf Rubys Rücken.

Talon rollte die Landkarte zusammen. Er steckte sie in den Rucksack mit den Vorräten und schaute dabei nach ihrem Stück vom Stein der Macht. An einer Seite war eine scharf gezackte Lücke. Dort fehlte noch ein Teil – oder sogar mehrere. Jedes Mal, wenn sie ein weiteres Stück gefunden hatten, verband es sich auf magische Weise mit den anderen und vergrößerte so den Stein.

Wie viele Teile es wohl noch gibt?, überlegte Talon.

Ruby schwang sich in die Luft.

Talon folgte ihr in Richtung Osten.

Die Freunde flogen, so schnell sie konnten. Still überlegten sie, was sie wohl beim Blubbernden Sumpf und beim Schlafsee vorfinden würden.

Der Blubbernde Sumpf

Als die Freunde sich dem Blubbernden Sumpf näherten, begannen ihre Augen zu tränen.

„Was ist denn das für ein furchtbarer Geruch?“, fragte Agila.

„Das ist der Sumpf!“, antwortete Talon und bedeckte den Schnabel mit seinem Flügel.

So weit das Auge reichte, erstreckte sich nichts als dicker, matschiger Morast.

Immer wieder stiegen riesige Blasen aus dem

Schlamm auf. Wenn sie platzten, hinterließen sie kleine Wolken aus stinkendem grünem Gas.

„Meine Augen brennen!“, rief Ruby.

„Meine auch!“, sagte Talon und blinzelte, um überhaupt noch etwas sehen zu können.

Rülps! Burps!, blubberte der Sumpf.

„Wir können nicht über das Moor fliegen!“, schrie Agila. „In den Blasen scheint irgendein Gift zu sein.“

„Folgt mir!“, rief Talon und flog ein Stück weiter Richtung Norden. Sie landeten am Rand des Blubbernden Sumpfes.

Agila hielt sich die Nase zu. „Was machen wir jetzt?“

Talon zog die Landkarte hervor. „Wir müssen uns noch weiter nördlich halten. Es wird länger dauern, als über den Sumpf zu fliegen, aber es ist die einzige Möglichkeit.“

„Wir müssen uns beeilen!“, erinnerte Ruby ihre Freunde.

Das ließ sich Agila nicht zweimal sagen und sprang auf den Rücken des Feuerfalken. Dann hoben sie ab und ließen den stinkenden Sumpf hinter sich.

Sie flogen viele Stunden lang. Kurz vor Sonnenuntergang erreichten sie den Schlafsee. Die Luft war frisch und das Wasser des Sees klar. Am Ufer fanden sie eine Gruppe Trauerweiden, deren lange Äste bis auf den Boden herabhingen.

„Seht mal", sagte Agila.

Sie schob ein paar Zweige zur Seite und verschwand hinter ihnen. Die Freunde folgten ihr.

„Das ist ein gutes Versteck", meinte Talon. Die dichten Blätter reichten so weit hinunter, dass sie die drei gut verbargen.

„Lasst uns hier unser Lager aufschlagen", schlug Agila vor.

„Burungs Spione werden uns hier nie finden", stimmte Ruby zu.

„Ist unser Stück vom Stein der Macht schon warm geworden?", fragte Agila. Normalerweise wurde es heiß und fing an zu glühen, wenn sie sich einem anderen Stück näherten.

Talon tastete im Rucksack herum. „Nein, es ist noch kalt", sagte er.

Ruby spähte zwischen den Zweigen hindurch und zeigte auf eine kleine Insel in der Mitte des Sees.

„Die sollten wir uns mal näher ansehen", meinte Talon. „Vielleicht ist dort das nächste Stück."

„Ich bleibe hier und baue uns Schlafplätze für heute Nacht", schlug Agila vor und sammelte einige dünne Zweige auf. Dann begann sie, Nester daraus zu flechten, auf denen sie schlafen konnten.

Währenddessen flogen Talon und Ruby zu der Insel. Sie war mit Bäumen und hohem Gras bewachsen, aber es war nichts von einem weiteren Stück des Steins der Macht zu sehen.

„Es ist nicht hier", sagte Ruby.

Talon schaute nach dem Stein im Rucksack. Er war immer noch kalt.

Der Mond stieg am Nachthimmel auf. Talon hoffte, dass keiner von Burungs Spionen sie beobachtete. Denn er wollte nicht, dass sie das nächste Stück vor ihnen fanden.

Talon tippte auf Rubys Flügel. „Das ist ein ziemlich großer See", sagte er. „Lass uns zum Lager zurückfliegen. Wir suchen morgen früh weiter."

Burung!

Talon und Ruby kehrten zum Lager zurück, als es gerade dunkel wurde.

„Wir sollten heute Nacht abwechselnd Wache halten“, schlug Agila vor.

„Gute Idee! Ich bin der Erste“, sagte Talon.

Er setzte seinen Rucksack ab und spähte durch eine kleine Lücke zwischen den Zweigen. Von Burungs Spionen war nichts zu sehen, aber früher oder später würden sie auftauchen.

Er schaute auf den Rucksack, der seinen Dolch, die Landkarte und ihr Stück vom Stein der Macht enthielt. Es war seine Aufgabe, den Stein – und seine Freunde – zu beschützen.

Ruby und Agila schnarchten leise. Die Zweige der Weide hielten sie verborgen, aber ein eisiger Wind blies durch die Blätter. Talon fröstelte, als es immer kälter wurde. Er wünschte, Ruby wäre wach, damit sie ihre Federn entzünden und sie alle drei wärmen könnte.

Die Stunden vergingen. Talon war müde, aber er wusste, dass er unbedingt wach bleiben musste. Plötzlich sah er eine schwarze Wolke, die sich allmählich auf den See zubewegte.

Der Schatten!, dachte Talon und sprang auf.

Blitze erfüllten den Himmel.

Die Blätter der Weide verfärbten sich braun und rieselten wie Staub zu Boden.

Ein großer Geier hockte zusammengekrümmt vor ihm!

BURUNG!

Talon kreischte erschrocken auf. Er wusste, dass er sich den Rucksack schnappen musste, aber er konnte sich nicht bewegen. Vor Angst zitterten seine Federn.

„Nun treffen wir uns doch noch", zischte der Geier mit einem bösen Grinsen, als er mit seinen scharfen Klauen nach dem Rucksack griff. „Ich denke, du hast etwas, das mir gehört."

Gerade noch rechtzeitig riss Talon den Sack aus seiner Reichweite. Burung knurrte.

Talon zog seinen Dolch heraus und hielt ihn Burung mit seinem zitternden Flügel entgegen.

„Burung ist da!", rief er seinen Freunden zu.

Augenblicklich waren die beiden wach.

Agila zielte mit ihrer Schleuder auf das verrunzelte Gesicht des Geiers. „Nicht bewegen!“, rief sie tapfer, obwohl auch ihre Pfoten zitterten.

Ruby breitete ihre Flügel aus. Ihre Federn fingen alle auf einmal an zu brennen. Die Flammen glühten rot und orange in der Dunkelheit.

Doch Burung schien keine Angst zu haben. „Deine Kräfte sind stärker, als ich dachte“, sagte er. „Stell dir mal vor, wie mächtig wir sein könnten, wenn wir uns zusammentun.“

„Niemals!“, schrie Ruby.

Schnell wie der Blitz griff Burung noch einmal nach Talons Rucksack. Seine spitzen Krallen rissen ihn auf und der Stein der Macht fiel heraus.

„Nein!“, schrie Talon.

Burung schnappte sich den Stein mit seinen scharfen Klauen und flog davon – über das Wasser auf das Schattenland zu.

Agila beschoss ihn vom Ufer aus mit Eicheln,

während die beiden anderen dem Geier in der Luft nachjagten. Ruby schleuderte Feuerbälle auf Burung. Einer davon traf ihn am Rücken. Er heulte auf und ließ den Stein der Macht los, der platschend ins Wasser fiel.

Burung schrie wütend auf und der Himmel war plötzlich voller Blitze. Der alte Geier stieß im Sturzflug zur Oberfläche des Sees herab, aber Ruby schleuderte weiter Feuerbälle auf ihn.

Burung schrie noch einmal auf und drehte sich zu den Freunden um.

„Es ist noch nicht vorbei!“, kreischte er. Dann flog er davon, auf die dunkle Wolke des *Schattens* zu.

Sobald Burung verschwunden war, segelte Talon über die Wasseroberfläche. Ruby kreiste über ihm und hielt Wache.

Aber es war zu spät. Der Stein der Macht war schon auf den Grund des Sees gesunken.

Plötzlich sah Talon einen blauen Blitz im Zickzack durchs Wasser schießen. Lange dunkle Schatten umringten den Stein und Hunderte rot leuchtender Augen blickten glänzend zu ihm hinauf.

Der verlorene Stein

Im Wasser sind Spione von Burung!", rief Talon. „Aale!"

Während er mit Ruby über dem See kreiste, beobachteten sie die blauen Lichtblitze, die von den Aalen ausgingen, und ihre glühenden roten Augen.

Britzel! Britzel!

„Was ist das für ein Geräusch?", fragte Talon. Ruby flog dichter über das Wasser.

BRITZEL! Das Geräusch wurde lauter und die

blauen Lichtblitze leuchteten heller. Ruby tauchte ihren Schnabel in den See.

„Autsch!“, schrie sie und stieg schnell wieder von der Wasseroberfläche auf.

„Es sind *Zitteraale*!“, sagte Talon.

Die beiden flogen zurück zum Ufer.

„Was ist da draußen passiert?“, fragte Agila, als Ruby sich den Schnabel rieb.

„Unser Stein liegt auf dem Grund des Sees“, antwortete sie.

„Und Burungs Spione bewachen ihn“, ergänzte Talon und verbarg sein Gesicht in den Flügeln.

Sie waren auf der Suche nach den Stücken des Steins der Macht schon so weit gekommen. Sie waren zur Feuerinsel, zu den Kristallhöhlen und zur Flüsternden Eiche gereist. Ihre drei Stücke hatten sich zu einem Stein verbunden – doch der war nun im Wasser verloren.

„Es war mein Fehler!“, jammerte Talon. „Ich hätte Burung davon abhalten müssen, unseren Stein zu stehlen. Nun sieht es so aus, als ob er ihn *und* das nächste Stück bekommen wird.“

Ruby stampfte mit dem Fuß auf. „Nein!“, rief sie.

Agila wandte sich an Talon. „Es war nicht dein Fehler, dass Burung unseren Stein gestohlen hat“, sagte sie. „Wir können ihn zurückholen. Ich weiß, dass wir es können.“

„Piep!“, stimmte Ruby zu.

Talon lächelte. „Okay“, sagte er. „Aber wie? Wenn wir das Wasser berühren, bekommen wir einen Stromschlag!“

„Und wenn wir einen Ast benutzen?“, schlug Ruby vor.

„Das wird nicht funktionieren“, antwortete Talon. „Ein Ast wäre nicht lang genug, um den Grund des Sees zu erreichen.“

Agila schaute zu den Weiden hinter ihnen. „Ich habe eine Idee!“, sagte sie.

Talon und Ruby folgten ihr zum Lager, wo sie schnell mit der Arbeit begann. Sie nahm sich eines der Schlafnester und verflocht die Zweige, Äste und Blätter so miteinander, dass eine neue Form entstand.

„Wir können nicht *ins* Wasser“, sagte Agila, „aber wir kommen dichter an den Stein heran, wenn wir *auf* dem Wasser sind.“

„Ein Floß!", sagte Talon, als er sah, was seine Freundin baute. „Damit können wir auf den See fahren."

„Aber wir brauchen immer noch etwas, um unter Wasser an den Stein zu kommen ...", sagte Ruby.

Agila zwinkerte ihr zu, dann brach sie einen langen, kräftigen Ast vom Baum ab. Sie verflocht einige Blätter zu einem Netz und befestigte es an einem Ende des Astes. Als sie fertig war, zeigte sie den beiden ihr Werk.

„Wer hat Lust, angeln zu gehen?", fragte sie.

Süße Träume

Als die Sonne über dem Schlafsee aufging, überprüfte Talon das Floß und das Netz.

„Das ist der perfekte Plan!", sagte er. „Ich werde zur Mitte des Sees fahren und unseren Stein holen."

Ruby schüttelte den Kopf. „Nein. Ich werde gehen."

„Du bist zu groß", erklärte ihr Talon. „Du wirst das Floß zum Sinken bringen. Und Agila hat Angst vor dem Wasser. Ich bin der Einzige, der es machen kann."

Ruby nickte.

„Denk daran: nicht das Wasser berühren", erinnerte ihn Agila. „Sonst bekommst du einen elektrischen Schlag."

Talon betrachtete das blaue Glimmen an der Oberfläche des Sees und erschauerte. „Keine Sorge, das mache ich nicht", sagte er.

Vorsichtig betrat er das Floß. Es hatte genau die richtige Größe für ihn. Agila gab ihm den selbst gebauten Kescher.

Ruby begleitete ihn ein Stück auf den See hinaus, dann flog sie zum Ufer zurück.

Talon schaute nach unten. Das Wasser war klar und er sah helle bunte Fische zwischen den Wasserpflanzen herumschwimmen.

Als sich das Floß der Mitte des Sees näherte, entdeckte Talon die langen hellblauen Gestalten der Zitteraale. Ihre Augen leuchteten bedrohlich unter Wasser, während sie ein purpurrotes Licht umkreisten.

Ich kann unseren Stein sehen!, dachte Talon. *Und er glüht!*

Er tauchte den Kescher ins Wasser. Die Aale machten unheimliche Geräusche und schossen unter ihm mit Lichtblitzen. Aber Talon ließ sich nicht ablenken und schob das Netz näher an den glühenden Stein am Boden des Sees heran.

Plötzlich tauchten Hunderte funkelnder goldener Lichter unter der Wasseroberfläche auf. Talon umfasste den Kescher noch fester und wünschte, er hätte seinen Dolch dabeigehabt. Doch dann schwebte ein leiser, zarter Gesang aus dem Wasser empor. Es hörte sich an wie das sanfte Plätschern von Regentropfen und war der allerschönste Klang, den Talon jemals gehört hatte. Die Lichter umringten die Aale und das Floß.

Die Fische trieben langsam davon, während Talon sich auf das Floß legte und dem Schlaflied zuhörte. Er schaute zu den bauschigen weißen Wolken am Himmel hinauf und der Kescher glitt aus seinem Flügel.

Bald darauf hatte er vergessen, dass er nach irgendetwas gesucht hatte, und war tief und fest eingeschlafen.

Nicht schon wieder!

Talon schreckte aus dem Schlaf auf. Die Sonne stand hoch oben am Himmel, was bedeutete, dass er stundenlang geschlafen hatte. Er war immer noch auf dem Floß, das inzwischen ans Ufer zurückgetrieben war. Talon konnte sich nicht erinnern, was er als Letztes getan hatte. Gähnend starrte er über den See.

Als er den Kescher neben sich sah, fiel ihm alles wieder ein.

Talon runzelte die Stirn. *Wie bin ich hierhergekommen? Wo sind Agila und Ruby?*, dachte er. *Oh nein! Hoffentlich ist Burung nicht zurückgekehrt, während ich geschlafen habe!*

Er flog am Ufer entlang und hielt Ausschau nach seinen Freunden.

Er fand sie in der Nähe, an einen Baumstumpf gelehnt.

Ruby schlief so fest, dass Talon laut rufen musste, um sie zu wecken.

Sie sprang auf und an ihren magischen Federn erschienen rot und orange leuchtende Flammen. „PIEP!"

„Ich bin es doch!", sagte Talon und wich vor ihren feurigen Flügeln zurück.

Rubys Federn hörten auf zu brennen.

Agila rieb sich die Augen. „Talon", sagte sie. „Was ist passiert?"

„Ich weiß es nicht genau. Eben war ich noch mitten auf dem See und schaute ins Wasser ... und im nächsten Moment war ich fest eingeschlafen. Und dann bin ich am Ufer wieder aufgewacht", sagte Talon. „Habt ihr gesehen, was passiert ist?"

Die beiden blickten sich an. „Wir sind auch eingeschlafen", gestand Agila.

„Ich bin immer noch schläfrig", gähnte Ruby.

Talon seufzte. „Ich schätze, wir haben letzte Nacht nicht viel Schlaf bekommen. Und wir haben gestern einen langen Weg zurückgelegt", sagte er.

Aber wie ist mein Floß wieder ans Ufer gekommen?, wunderte er sich.

„Hast du unseren Stein gefunden?", fragte Ruby.

Talon schüttelte den Kopf und runzelte die Stirn. Er glaubte, ihren Stein im Wasser gesehen zu haben, aber nun war er sich nicht mehr so sicher. Er ging zum Floß zurück. „Lasst es uns noch einmal versuchen. Ich bin nicht mehr müde."

Ruby lotste das Floß zurück in die Mitte des Sees. Talon schaute über den Rand und suchte nach ihrem Stein. Das blaue Licht der Aale flimmerte um ihn herum.

Doch wieder begannen Hunderte winziger goldener Lichter im Wasser zu glitzern und die Fische trieben davon. Dann hörte Talon dieselbe sanfte Musik wie zuvor über den See schweben.

Dieses Lied habe ich doch schon mal gehört, dachte Talon, als er in einen tiefen Schlaf fiel.

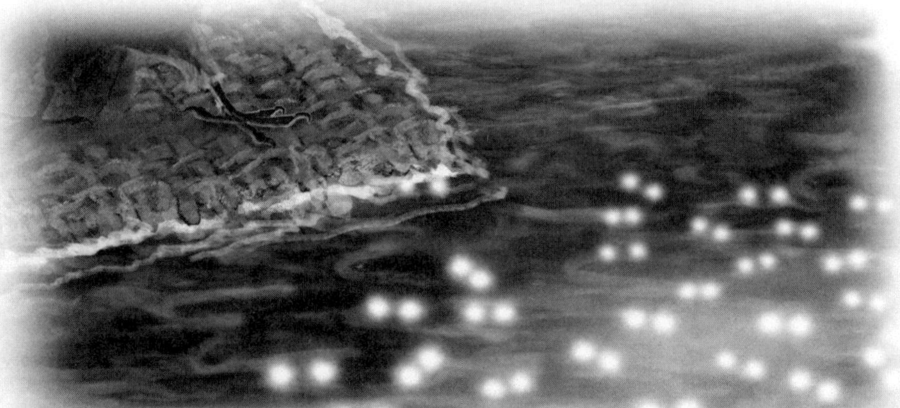

Das Schlaflied

Wieder wachte Talon am Ufer des Sees auf und rieb sich die Augen. *Hier geht eindeutig etwas Merkwürdiges vor!*, dachte er.

Seine Freunde schliefen wieder tief und fest.

„Aufwachen!", schrie Talon.

„Huch?!" Agila sprang hoch und ergriff ihre Schleuder.

„Hast du den Stein gefunden?", fragte Ruby.

„Nein", sagte Talon. „Ich habe wieder goldene

Lichter im Wasser gesehen und ein seltsames Lied gehört. Dann bin ich eingeschlafen."

Agilas Augen wurden groß. „Ich habe auch Musik gehört!"

„Ich auch!", fügte Ruby hinzu.

„Ich weiß nicht, was hier los ist. Aber wir müssen weiterversuchen, unseren Stein wiederzubekommen", sagte Talon. „Burung wird bald zurückkehren."

Haaaa! Haaaa! Haaaa!

Die Freunde hörten ein träges Lachen.

„Schaut mal, da oben!", sagte Ruby.

Ein haariges graues Faultier hing an einem Ast über ihnen.

„Ihr könnt es ruhig weiterversuchen“, sagte es langsam. „Aber ihr werdet immer wieder da enden, wo ihr angefangen habt.“

Agila zielte mit ihrer Schleuder auf das Faultier. „Arbeitest du für Burung?“, fragte sie misstrauisch.

Talon betrachtete prüfend die Augen des Faultiers. Sie waren braun. „Er ist kein Spion von Burung“, flüsterte er.

Agila senkte ihre Schleuder. „Ich bin Agila. Das sind Talon und Ruby.“

„Ich bin Fred", sagte das Faultier. „Freut mich, euch kennenzulernen."

„Also, Fred, warum glaubst du, dass es uns nicht gelingen wird?", fragte Agila.

„Weil ihr von den Feen ausgetrickst werdet", antwortete das Faultier.

„Was für Feen?", fragte Ruby.

„Wasserfeen", erwiderte Fred. „Sie beschützen den See."

„Wir wollen dem See keinen Schaden zufügen. Wir suchen nur etwas, das dort hineingefallen ist. Und wir müssen es so schnell wie möglich zurückhaben", erklärte Agila.

Talon erinnerte sich, dass er gesehen hatte, wie der Stein am Grund des Sees glühte.

Das tat er immer, wenn das nächste Stück in der Nähe war. *Das kann nur bedeuten, dass das neue Stück ebenfalls im See ist!* Er fragte das Faultier: „Gab es schon einen magischen Stein im See, bevor wir hierhergekommen sind? Ist es das, was die Feen beschützen?“

Fred schüttelte langsam seinen Kopf. „Ich weiß nur, dass die Feen singen, wenn sie Gefahr spüren. Euer Stein ist im See in Sicherheit. Niemand kann ihrem Gesang widerstehen – nicht einmal Burungs Spione.“

Der See begann zu glitzern und ein Schlaflied klang über das Wasser.

Fred gähnte. „Selbst ich nicht …“, fügte er hinzu.

Talon ließ die Federn hängen. *Nun werden wir*

unseren Stein niemals zurückbekommen. Und wir werden niemals das nächste Stück finden …

Eingelullt von der sanften Musik sanken die Freunde zu Boden und schlossen müde ihre Augen.

Angriff!

Talon lief unruhig am Ufer auf und ab.

„Es *muss* einen Weg für uns geben, an den Stein heranzukommen, ohne einzuschlafen", sagte er. „Wir müssen unsere Ohren vor der Musik der Wasserfeen verschließen."

„Aber was machen wir denn bloß, wenn die Aale unseren Stein inzwischen schon haben?", fragte Agila.

„Ich glaube, dass sie ihn auch nicht erreichen

können“, antwortete Talon. „Du hast ja gehört, was Fred gesagt hat – selbst Burungs Spione können dem Gesang der Feen nicht widerstehen.“

„Burung wird bald zurück sein“, sagte Agila und zeigte auf die dunkle Wolke des *Schattens* in der Ferne.

„Er darf sich nicht noch einmal an uns heranschleichen“, sagte Talon entschlossen.

In diesem Moment hörten die Freunde das Flattern vieler Flügel über ihnen. Große gestreifte

Kreaturen kreisten in der Luft und schnappten mit ihren langen scharfen Schnäbeln.

Klack! Klack! Klack!

„Tiger-Fledermäuse!“, rief Talon und zog seinen Dolch.

Schnell duckten sich die drei hinter eine Weide.

Plötzlich wurde der See von Hunderten goldener

Lichter erleuchtet. Er glitzerte hell, als die Tiger-Fledermäuse dicht über das Wasser segelten.

„Ich glaube nicht, dass sie nach uns suchen“, flüsterte Talon.

„Aber was wollen sie dann?“, fragte Agila, als sie die Fledermäuse in der Nähe am Ufer landen sah.

Eine der Tiger-Fledermäuse hielt etwas Kleines, Helles in ihrem langen Schnabel. Es schimmerte golden in der Dunkelheit.

Die Freunde krochen dichter heran, um besser sehen zu können. Das leuchtende Etwas stieß einen leisen Schrei aus.

Talon schnappte nach Luft. „Ich glaube, sie haben eine Fee gefangen!“

Nova

Wir müssen die Fee retten!", sagte Talon. Er ergriff seinen Dolch und stürzte auf die Tiger-Fledermäuse zu.

Agila folgte ihm und schoss mit Eicheln. **Boing!** Sie traf die Tiger-Fledermaus, die die Fee festhielt, und das winzige Wesen fiel auf den Boden.

Ruby schrie laut: „**Aiiiiii-iiie!**"

Burungs Spione hielten sich die Ohren zu. Der Feuerfalke schleuderte kleine Flammen auf die

Tiger-Fledermäuse. Die kreischten auf und flogen davon.

„Das wird sie lehren, sich nicht mit uns anzulegen!“, sagte Agila lachend.

Talon flatterte hinüber zur Fee. Ihre Augen waren geschlossen und ihre Flügel nass und zerknittert.

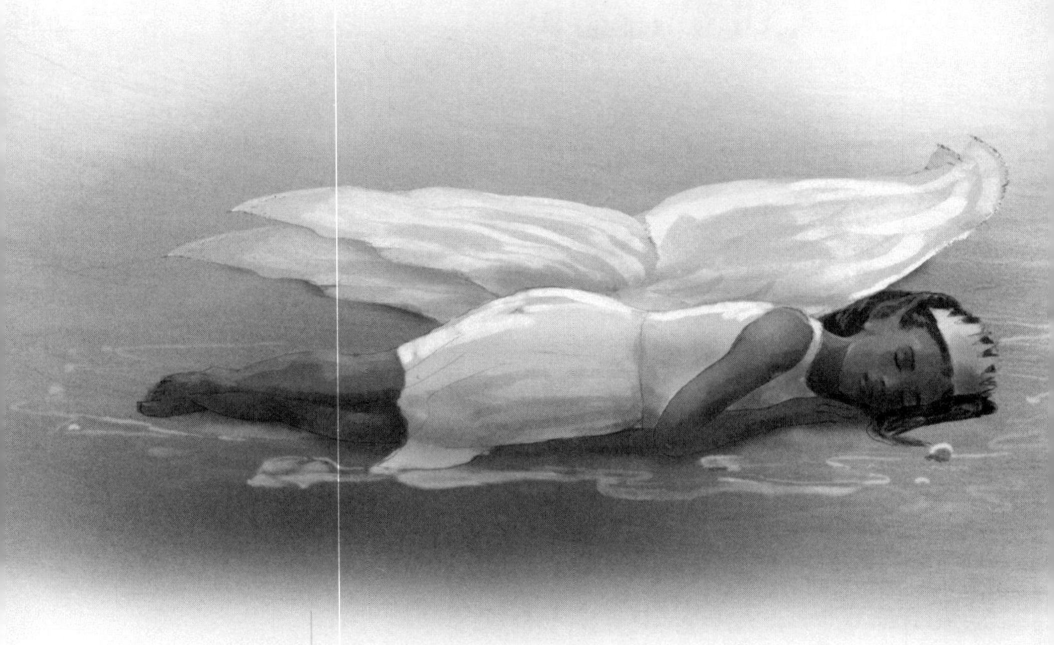

„Oh, nein!“, rief Ruby.

„Geht es ihr gut?“, fragte Agila.

Talon beugte sich über die kleine Fee. Sie war nicht viel größer als ein Schmetterling. Ihr Gesicht war blass und ihr heller Schein flackerte.

Ruby piepste betrübt, als Talon das kleine Wesen aufhob.

Agila legte Talon die Pfote auf die Schulter. „Burung wollte wohl versuchen, mithilfe einer Fee an den Stein heranzukommen", sagte sie.

Plötzlich öffnete die Fee erst ein Auge und dann das andere. Sie setzte sich auf und fragte: „Sind sie weg?"

Talon nickte.

„Puh!“, sagte die Fee mit einem Grinsen. Sie stand auf und schlug mit den Flügeln. Ihr Körper leuchtete jetzt wieder hell und golden. „Danke, dass ihr mich gerettet habt!“

„Gern geschehen“, sagte Talon. „Jeder Feind der Tiger-Fledermäuse ist unser Freund.“

Die Fee schaute zu den drei Freunden hoch, die über ihr aufragten. Als sie Ruby erblickte, machte sie große Augen.

„Das ist Ruby“, erklärte Talon ihr. „Sie ist ein Feuerfalke. Ich bin Talon und das ist Agila.“ Er streckte einen Flügel aus, um ihre winzige Hand zu schütteln.

„Ich bin Nova", sagte die Fee. Sie schaute Ruby skeptisch an. „Ein Feuerfalke? Ich dachte, ihr lebt alle im Verborgenen."

Ruby öffnete ihren Schnabel, um die Fee zu fragen, was sie damit meinte, aber –

Über ihnen waren Flügelschläge zu hören.

„Die Tiger-Fledermäuse sind zurück!", schrie Agila.

„Lauft!", rief Talon und rannte auf die Bäume zu.

Magie unter dem Wasser

Talon, Agila, Ruby und Nova versteckten sich unter den Ästen der Weide.

Klack! Klack! Klack!

Talon hielt die Luft an, während er dem Schnappen der Schnäbel am Himmel über ihnen lauschte.

Nach einer Weile flatterten die Tiger-Fledermäuse davon.

„Puh!“, seufzte Nova erleichtert. Sie strahlte ihre neuen Freunde an. „Also, warum seid ihr zum

Schlafsee gekommen?“, fragte sie und schwirrte um Talons Kopf herum.

„Wir sind auf einer langen Reise, um alle Stücke des Steins der Macht zu finden“, erklärte Talon ihr. „Unsere magische Landkarte hat uns hierher geleitet, aber dann ist Burung aufgetaucht.“

„Er hat versucht, unseren Stein zu stehlen, aber dabei hat er ihn in den See fallen lassen“, ergänzte Ruby.

„Also *deswegen* ist Burung zu unserem See gekommen!“, sagte Nova. „Wir wussten, dass etwas Seltsames vor sich geht, als die Zitteraale wie durch einen Zauber hier erschienen sind."

„Tut mir leid", erwiderte Talon.

„Wir haben mehrmals versucht, unseren Stein zurückzubekommen. Aber wir haben es nicht geschafft, an Burungs Spionen, den Zitteraalen, vorbeizukommen", sagte Agila.

„Außerdem lassen du und deine Freunde uns immer wieder einschlafen", fügte Talon hinzu.

Nova errötete. „Entschuldigung", sagte sie. „Aber wir müssen *unser* Stück vom Stein der Macht beschützen." Erschrocken schlug sie die Hand vor den Mund.

Also habe ich unseren Stein tatsächlich glühen sehen!, dachte Talon.

Er hat geglüht, weil er nahe bei einem der anderen Teile war!

„Ihr habt also das nächste Stück! Wo ist es?“, fragte Talon mit großen Augen.

„Mein Vater wird euch alles erklären“, erwiderte Nova und zeigte zum Wasser. „Ich werde euch zu ihm bringen – auf den Grund des Sees.“

„Aber ich kann nicht schwimmen!“, schrie Agila.

„Du brauchst nicht zu schwimmen“, beruhigte Nova sie lachend.

„Was ist mit den Aalen? Und den Tiger-Fledermäusen? Ich bin sicher, dass sie noch in der Nähe sind“, wandte Talon ein.

Novas Flügel glühten. „Überlasst das mir.“

Sie flog zu einem Baum und pflückte eine Handvoll weicher Blüten.

„Steckt sie in eure Ohren“, sagte sie.

Talon, Ruby und Agila stopften sich die flauschigen Blüten in die Ohren. Talon sah, wie Nova ihren Mund öffnete und zu singen begann. Ihre Flügel glühten heller.

Die Tiger-Fledermäuse kamen wie hypnotisiert unter einem Baum auf der anderen Seite des Sees hervor. Dann sanken sie laut schnarchend zu Boden. Nova hörte auf zu singen und gab den Freunden ein Zeichen, dass sie die Blüten herausnehmen konnten.

„Folgt mir“, sagte sie und flog zum Ufer.

Ihre Flügel schimmerten in einem zarten Rosa. Als sie die Hände ausstreckte, stiegen winzige, glitzernde Funken auf, die zu vier glänzenden Blasen wurden. Sie wuchsen und wuchsen, bis sie so groß wie Ruby waren.

Nova zeigte auf die Blasen. „Die werden uns in die Tiefe des Sees bringen."

Talon kratzte sich am Kopf. „Und wie?", fragte er.

Blubb!

„Genau so!" Die Fee lachte über Ruby, die einfach in eine der Blasen hineingegangen war. Dann machte sie es dem Feuerfalken nach.

„Piep!" Ruby lächelte.

Talon machte einen Schritt vorwärts. **Blubb!** „Was ist, wenn sie unter Wasser platzt?", rief Agila aus ihrer Blase heraus.

„Das wird sie nicht“, versprach die Fee.

Talons Magen schlug Purzelbäume, als sie sich in die Luft erhoben.

Die Freunde schwebten ein Stück über den See und sanken dann langsam unter Wasser.

Im Reich der Wasserfeen

Der See war tiefer, als Talon gedacht hatte. Es fühlte sich an, als würde er wie ein Stein auf den Grund sinken. In Wirklichkeit glitt er langsam immer weiter nach unten. Kleine goldene Lichter umringten sie und begleiteten sie auf ihrem Weg zum Grund des Sees.

Talon schaute zu seinen Freunden hinüber. Ihre Blasen waren voller Luft – sodass sie unter Wasser atmen konnten. Zwischen den Wasserpflanzen schwammen bunte Fische herum. Ruby winkte einem von ihnen zu, doch der kümmerte sich gar nicht um sie und glitt einfach vorbei.

Agila sah gar nicht glücklich aus. Ihr Schwanz zuckte hin und her und sie hielt sich ihre Pfoten vor die Augen.

„Zitteraale!“, schrie Ruby plötzlich und zeigte mit dem Flügel dorthin.

Talon konnte rote Augen aus dem Schilf spähen sehen.

Nova machte den Freunden ein Zeichen, sich die Blüten wieder in die Ohren zu stecken. Dann öff- nete sie den Mund und begann zu singen. Die Aale trieben schnell davon und die Freunde nahmen die Blüten wieder heraus.

Kurz darauf entdeckte Talon ein weiteres schimmerndes Licht auf dem Grund des Sees. Golden und silbern glitzerte es durch das Wasser zu ihnen herauf.

Während sie näher heranglitten, wurde das Licht immer größer. Bald schwebten ihre bunt schillernden Blasen über einer gigantischen Kuppel ganz unten auf dem Grund des Schlafsees. In ihrer Mitte stand ein riesiger silbern glänzender Palast.

„Hier lebst du also?“, fragte Talon mit großen Augen.

„Willkommen im Reich der Wasserfeen!“, sagte Nova.

Ein königlicher Empfang

Auf einmal sanken die vier Blasen mit den Freunden durch die große Kuppel in das Feenreich hinein.

Sie schwebten bis zum Boden.

Dann –

Plopp!

Als die Blasen platzten, versprühten sie ringsherum glitzernde Funken.

Agila hielt sich immer noch die Augen zu.

„Schau dir doch mal diese unglaubliche Unterwasserwelt an", sagte Talon.

Agila nahm die Pfoten herunter und schnappte nach Luft. „Dein Zuhause ist so wunderschön, Nova!", sagte sie.

„Ja, es ist fantastisch!", stimmte Ruby zu.

Talon betrachtete staunend das Unterwasser-Königreich. Es gab kleine weiße Häuser und einen großen Palast aus Elfenbein in der Mitte. Überall, wohin Talon schaute, sah er Feen, die herumflatterten und sich vergnügten.

Da die große Kuppel durchsichtig war, konnte er die Fische und Pflanzen im See sehen.

Als einige Feen in der Nähe anfingen zu singen, hielt Ruby sich die Ohren zu. „Nicht mehr schlafen!“, rief sie.

„Keine Sorge“, sagte Nova. „Nur ein besonderes magisches Lied kann euch in das Reich der Träume schicken.“

Agila stemmte ihre Pfoten in die Hüften. „Und warum habt ihr das mit uns gemacht?“, fragte sie.

„Habt ihr etwa gedacht, dass wir Spione von Burung sind?“, fügte Talon hinzu.

„Uns wurde gesagt, wir sollten *niemanden* in die Nähe des Sees lassen. Das wäre zu gefährlich. Burung und seine Spione sind zu dicht an den –" Nova zögerte. „Mein Vater wird es euch erklären. Folgt mir."

Sie folgten Nova zu dem großen, funkelnden Tor des Palastes.

Zwei Feen mit silbernen Rüstungen öffneten die Türen. „Willkommen zu Hause, Prinzessin Nova", begrüßten die Wächter sie.

Talons Unterkiefer klappte herunter. „Prinzessin?", fragte er.

„Ich hätte es euch sagen sollen, nachdem ihr mich vor den Tiger-Fledermäusen gerettet habt", sagte Nova.

„Tiger-Fledermäuse?", dröhnte eine Stimme.

Der Feenkönig mit seiner glänzenden Krone flog durch die Halle auf sie zu. Sein langes goldenes Gewand hing bis auf den Boden.

Nova errötete. „Die Tiger-Fledermäuse hatten mich entführt“, sagte sie. „Aber meine neuen Freunde haben mich gerettet. Das sind Talon, Ruby und Agila.“

„Danke, dass ihr meine Tochter gerettet habt“, sagte Novas Vater. „Ich bin König Nidus.“

Er sah jeden von ihnen lächelnd an. Als sein Blick auf Ruby fiel, machte er große Augen. „Ein Feuerfalke!“, rief er und verbeugte sich vor ihr. „Ich dachte, ihr seid alle verschwunden!“

„Ich bin der letzte Feuerfalke“, erklärte ihm Ruby.

Der Feenkönig hob seine Hände. Über ihnen tauchten funkelnde Lichter auf und füllten die Luft mit glitzernder Magie.

In der Mitte der großen Halle erschien ein langer Tisch, der mit Bergen von Speisen bedeckt war.

„Wir werden ein Fest zu deinen Ehren geben!“, verkündete der König Ruby. „Und um euch allen zu danken, dass ihr Nova gerettet habt.“

Agila grinste. „Ich verhungere gleich!“, sagte sie.

Talon stieß sie mit dem Ellbogen an. „Vielen Dank, Eure Majestät", sagte er zum König.

Die drei Freunde verbeugten sich. Dann eilten sie hinüber zum Tisch.

Agila ergriff eine Handvoll Weintrauben, während Talon seinen Schnabel in eine Schüssel mit einer blubbernden hellgrünen Suppe tauchte. Einige Feen gesellten sich zu ihnen, aßen und plauderten miteinander.

„Also, was führt euch in mein Reich?", fragte König Nidus.

Talon wandte sich zu ihm. „Wir suchen nach allen Stücken des Steins der Macht."

Das Lächeln des Königs verschwand.

„Wir müssen ihn wieder zusammensetzen, um damit Burung zu bekämpfen", fuhr Talon fort. „Ohne den Stein der Macht können wir Perodia nicht retten. Gestern ist unser Stück in den See gefallen. Nova sagte, dass ihr auch eines besitzt. Wir hatten gehofft, dass ihr uns helfen könnt."

Es wurde ganz still in der Halle, als der König vor Talons Gesicht flog. Er sah ihn böse an. „Diese Steine gehören uns“, sagte der König. „Ihr könnt sie nicht haben.“

König Nidus

Nova flog zu ihrem Vater.

„Bitte, Papa – Talon, Agila und Ruby haben mich gerettet", sagte sie. „Du kannst ihnen vertrauen."

Der König runzelte die Augenbrauen, während er angestrengt nachdachte. Dann schaute er sie ernst an. „Na gut. Deine Freunde können *ihr* Stück vom Stein der Macht mitnehmen. Aber die Feuerfalken haben die einzelnen Teile in ganz Perodia versteckt, um sie in Sicherheit zu bringen. Und sie haben darauf vertraut, dass wir *unser* Stück beschützen", erklärte er ihr. „Es muss hier im Palast bleiben."

„Aber Vater", sagte Nova. „Ich bin sicher, dass Burungs Spione ihm in der Zwischenzeit alles berichtet haben. Er weiß also, dass sich zwei Stücke des Steins in unserem See befinden. Unseres und das meiner Freunde. Er wird noch mehr Spione zu uns schicken. Sie haben heute schon versucht, mich zu entführen. Ich bin sicher, dass das nur der Anfang

war. Burung wird nicht ruhen, bis er beide Stücke hat."

Agila trat vor. „Könnt ihr Burung nicht einfach einschlafen lassen, wenn er versucht, in den See einzudringen?", fragte sie.

Nova runzelte die Stirn. „Sein mächtiger dunkler Zauber ermöglicht es ihm, unserem magischen Schlaflied zu widerstehen."

Talon wandte sich an den König. „Wenn ihr uns beide Stücke gebt, wird Burung euch vielleicht in Ruhe lassen", sagte er.

Der König schüttelte wieder den Kopf. „Er wird niemals aufhören. Das hat er früher schon bewiesen. Aber ihr könnt unser Stück nicht haben", sagte er. „Nun folgt mir. Ich werde euch zu eurem Stein bringen."

Die Freunde folgten Nova und König Nidus vorsichtig eine Wendeltreppe hinunter und dann einen Flur entlang, der zu einer großen, silbernen Tür führte.

Der König zog einen goldenen Schlüssel heraus und steckte ihn in das Schlüsselloch.

Als sich die Tür öffnete, drang ein helles purpurrotes Licht heraus.

Das nächste Stück

Ruby hüpfte auf und ab. „Der Stein der Macht!", jubelte sie.

Auf einem Tisch in der Mitte des Raumes stand ein Glaskasten. Darin befand sich ein kleines, gezacktes Stück des Steins.

„Das ist das neue Stück, das wir gesucht haben!", rief Talon aus.

„Wie ich euch schon gesagt habe, könnt ihr es nicht haben", sagte König Nidus nachdrücklich.

„Ich habe den Feuerfalken versprochen, es mit meinem Leben zu beschützen."

Ruby trat vor. „Ich *bin* ein Feuerfalke", sagte sie. „Der Stein der Macht gehört zu mir."

Der König lief auf und ab, als er über das nachdachte, was Ruby gesagt hatte. Talon konnte spüren, dass der König sich verpflichtet fühlte, sein Stück vom Stein der Macht zu behalten.

„Ähm ...", unterbrach Agila die Stille. „Wo ist eigentlich *unser* Stein?"

Nova öffnete eine große Holztruhe, die unter dem Tisch stand. Sie half ihrem Vater, einen Kasten aus Kristall herauszuheben, der größer war als die beiden zusammen.

Beide Teile des Steins glühten hell, weil sie so dicht beieinander waren.

„Nachdem euer Stück in den See gefallen war, haben wir es hierhergebracht", erklärte Nova ihnen.

„Danke, dass ihr es sicher aufbewahrt habt", sagte Talon.

Agila stupste ihn sanft an. „Wir müssen die Teile unbedingt zusammensetzen, um zu wissen, ob wir jetzt alle Stücke haben“, flüsterte sie.

Talon nickte, dann wandte er sich dem Feenkönig zu. „König Nidus, ich habe eine Idee. Ich glaube, dass wir beweisen können, dass die Stücke zusammengehören – und dass Ruby sie bekommen sollte.“

Der König runzelte die Stirn. „Und wie?“, fragte er.

Talon zeigte auf den Glaskasten. „Lasst Ruby die Steine halten.“

Der König schüttelte den Kopf. „Sie sind sehr heiß! Unser Stück begann zu glühen, als euer Stein in unser Königreich gebracht wurde. Wir benutzen unsere stärkste Magie, um zu verhindern, dass sie den Palast niederbrennen“, erklärte er ihnen.

„Die Steine können mich nicht verletzen“, sagte Ruby.

„Die Stücke vom Stein der Macht glühen, wenn sie nahe beieinander sind – oder bei Ruby“, setzte Agila hinzu.

Der König hob den Deckel des Glaskastens an, während Talon den Kristallkasten öffnete.

Warmes purpurfarbenes Licht breitete sich im ganzen Raum aus.

Ruby nahm die Stücke heraus und legte sie nebeneinander auf den Tisch.

Beide Teile begannen zu zittern. Ein lautes Summen erfüllte den Raum und dann bewegten sie sich wackelnd aufeinander zu. In einer Explosion aus hellem purpurrotem Licht verbanden sie sich miteinander und wurden zu einem Stein.

„Seht nur!", rief Talon und zeigte auf eine kleine gezackte Lücke an der Seite des Steins. „Es fehlt nur noch ein Stück!"

Ruby und Agila sprangen begeistert auf und ab.

König Nidus strich mit der Hand durch die Luft und hinterließ dabei eine Spur aus glitzerndem Staub. Der Stein hob sich vom Tisch und schwebte hinüber zu Ruby.

„Du hast recht", sagte König Nidus. „Ich sehe ein, dass der Stein der Macht zu euch gehört. Ich vertraue darauf, dass ihr gut auf ihn achtgebt."

„Das werden wir", versprach Ruby.

Sie steckte den glühenden Stein in Talons

Rucksack, aber er fiel durch das Loch, das Burung mit seiner scharfen Klaue hineingerissen hatte.

„Ich werde das reparieren“, sagte Nova. Sie streute goldenen Staub darüber und verschloss so das Loch. Dann schwebte der Stein zurück in den Rucksack.

„Danke“, sagte Talon.

Der König lächelte. „Ich hätte nicht gedacht, dass ich noch einmal einen Feuerfalken treffen würde“, sagte er. „Es war so schön, euch kennenzulernen – euch alle. Und nochmals danke dafür, dass ihr meine Tochter gerettet habt.“

Die Freunde verbeugten sich vor dem König.

„Schlaft heute Nacht im Palast“, fuhr er fort. „Es ist sicherer für euch, wenn ihr am Morgen aufbrecht.“

„Vielen Dank“, antwortete Talon. „Wir werden bei Sonnenaufgang abreisen.“

Zurück nach Hause

Am nächsten Morgen schien Sonnenlicht durch das Fenster ihres Schlafzimmers.

„Es ist Zeit aufzubrechen“, sagte Talon. „Wir müssen uns beeilen, für den Fall, dass Burung oder seine Spione auf uns warten.“

Agila hielt ihre Schleuder hoch. „Wenn sie da sind, werden wir bereit sein.“

Rubys Federn funkelten hell. „Von mir aus kann's losgehen“, sagte sie.

Nova wartete vor dem Palast auf ihre Freunde. „Seid ihr euch sicher, dass ihr nicht bei uns bleiben wollt?“, fragte sie. „Hier seid ihr außer Gefahr.“

Talon schüttelte den Kopf. „Wir müssen das letzte Stück vom Stein der Macht finden“, sagte er. „Es ist der einzige Weg, Perodia zu retten.“

„Ich verstehe“, sagte Nova. Sie seufzte tief. „Bereit?“, fragte sie.

Talon nickte.

Novas Feenflügel erglühten in einem sanften Rosa. Sie streckte ihre Hände aus. Wieder stiegen winzige, glitzernde Funken auf und wurden zu drei glänzenden Blasen.

Talon, Agila und Ruby traten mit einem lauten **Blubb, Blubb, Blubb!** hinein. Sie winkten Nova zu, während die schimmernden Blasen langsam nach oben schwebten.

„Viel Glück!", rief Nova. „Wenn ihr einmal Hilfe braucht, ruft einfach in die Muschel hinein." Sie zeigte auf eine große Muschel, die auf magische Weise vor Talons Füßen erschienen war. Er hob sie auf und steckte sie in den Rucksack.

Hunderte kleiner goldener Lichter schwebten um die drei Freunde herum und trugen sie bis zur Oberfläche.

Plopp!

Ihre Blasen platzten am Ufer und versprühten ringsherum glitzernde Funken.

Talon blickte zum Himmel. Er war klar und von Burung oder seinen Spionen war nichts zu sehen.

„Wo müssen wir jetzt hin?“, fragte Agila.

Talon zog die Landkarte heraus und legte den Stein darauf. Ein kleiner glänzender Punkt erschien auf der Karte. Ruby schnappte nach Luft, als sie über Talons Schulter schaute.

„Der Wald von Valor!“, rief Agila.

„Das nächste Stück ist da, wo wir gestartet sind“, sagte Talon. Er sah seine Freunde an. „Wir kehren nach Hause zurück. Es ist Zeit, Burung ein für alle Mal zu stoppen.“

Katrina Charman wollte Kinderbuchautorin werden, seit sie elf war. Damals forderte ihr Lehrer die Klasse auf, ein Nachwort zu Roald Dahls Buch *Matilda* zu schreiben. Katrinas Lehrer fand ihren Text gut genug, um ihn an Roald Dahl persönlich zu schicken. Leider hat sie nie eine Antwort erhalten, aber dieses Erlebnis entfachte ihre Liebe zum Lesen und Schreiben. Katrina lebt mit ihrem Mann und ihren drei Töchtern in England.

Jeremy Norton ist ein erfahrener Illustrator und Maler. Schon als Kind war er ein fantasievoller und produktiver Künstler und er versucht nach wie vor, in seinen Arbeiten ein Gespür für das Wunderbare zu vermitteln. Jeremy Norton lebt in Spanien. *Der letzte Feuerfalke* ist seine erste Reihe für Leseanfänger.

Das will ich lesen!

Band 3

ISBN 978-3-7432-0814-8

Die Zeit drängt – Burungs finstere Magie breitet sich weiter über Perodia aus. Talon, Agila und Ruby müssen sich beeilen, um das nächste Stück des Steins der Macht zu finden. Auf ihrem Weg zur flüsternden Eiche werden die drei Freunde von einem gefährlichen Sandsturm überrascht. Werden sie es schaffen, ihm zu entkommen und den Stein vor Burungs Spionen zu retten?

Loewe
Das will ich lesen!

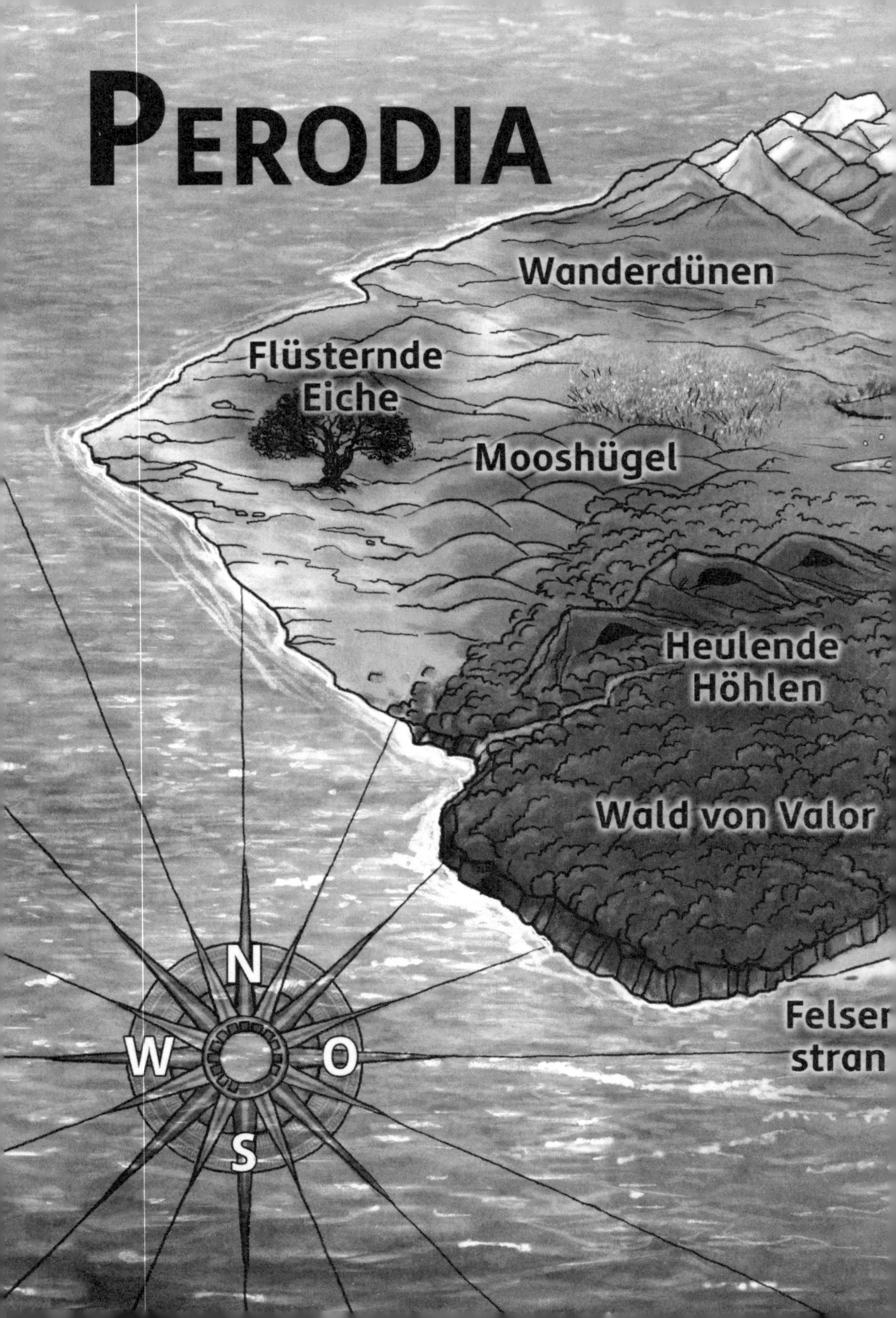
PERODIA
Wanderdünen
Flüsternde Eiche
Mooshügel
Heulende Höhlen
Wald von Valor
Felsen
stran
N
W
O
S